Seasonings Cookbook

Seasonings Cookbook for Quantity Cuisine

Edited by JULE WILKINSON

CBI PUBLISHING COMPANY, INC.
51 Sleeper Street
Boston, Massachusetts 02210

Text Designer: Bywater Production Services
Production Editor: Linda Dunn McCue
Compositor: J & L Typographics
Cover Designer: Betsy Franklin
Cover Photo: American Spice Trade Association

Library of Congress Cataloging in Publication Data

Main entry under title:

Seasonings cookbook for quantity cuisine.

    Bibliography: p.
    Includes index.
    1. Condiments. 2. Spices. 3. Quantity
cookery.
I. Wilkinson, Jule.
TX819.A1S36   641.6′384   80-14412
ISBN 0-8436-2188-5

Printing (*last digit*): 9 8 7 6 5 4 3 2 1

Printed in the United States of America

List of contributors

North Atlantic Seafood Association
National Fisheries Institute
Shrimp Association of the Americas
General Foods
National Peanut Council
Angostura Aromatic Bitters
Lea & Perrins, Inc.
Florida Tomato Exchange
Florida Celery Committee
American Mushroom Institute
American Spice Trade Association

Contents

Introduction

What *is* a seasoning?

Webster's very broadly defines a seasoning as "something that serves to season; *esp*: an ingredient (as a condiment, spice, or herb) added to food primarily for the savor that it imparts." This simple definition is as good a one as can be found, and we have consequently used it as our guide in deciding which products to include and which not to include in this text.

The key to the definition's usefulness is the word, "primarily." For a book about seasonings could conceivably have included a discussion of every edible substance known to humankind. Theoretically, in any given recipe, anything which contributes flavor could be called a seasoning. Defining the term this broadly, however, would have so diluted the meaning of the word as to have made the text of questionable value to the professional chef.

This book concentrates rather on products or ingredients which are added to foods *primarily* for the savor they impart. They are products used principally as flavorings or seasonings and not foods which *incidentally* contribute some flavor to the finished dish. For instance, when discussing fruits as seasonings, we include citrus rinds, juices, and extracts, because these are added to a dish primarily to impart flavor. We have not included discussion of whole fruits. While whole fruits are naturally flavorful, their primary function is as foodstuffs, not as ingredients used to add flavor or enhance the taste of a completed dish.

Similarly, we include various cheeses that are used to add flavor to particular recipes, but do not discuss the merits of individual cheeses as separate and distinct foods.

What kinds of ingredients are generally used as seasonings? Keeping in mind our basic definition, we have included spices (any of the various aromatic vegetable products such as pepper or cinnamon), herbs (seed-producing plants with no woody tissue such as the basils or coriander), cheeses, dehydrated onion and garlic, flavoring extracts, wines, cordials, liqueurs, and ingredients made from combinations of some or all of these products.

We have also tried to be reasonable about availability in deciding what items to include and which to exclude. While some products listed in our glossary may be hard to find, most will be available through normal foodservice supply channels. The criterion of availability ruled out our including many of the more esoteric spices and herbs, available only from highly specialized sources. We have mentioned only those more difficult to find items about which we've been asked numerous questions over the years.

The recipes in this text have been arranged with clarity and convenience foremost in mind. You will find recipes grouped into the traditional categories of appetizers, soups, meats, and so forth, allowing you to go directly to the *kind* of dish you wish to prepare and then to select among the rich varieties of individual recipes within each category. Each recipe also includes a "featured seasoning" section, highlighting the kinds of seasonings that contribute to the distinctive flavor of the dish.

While there have been countless texts and cookbooks on spices and herbs—even encyclopedic works on the broader subject of flavor—this is the first text that looks at seasoning from the professional chef's point of view, illustrating the rich and exciting world of seasoning with practical, working recipes.

The quantity recipes which begin on page 29 have been chosen with one common denominator in mind—in each, seasoning is its genius. And because there is such a wealth of innovative seasoning ideas from other lands, the recipes have been collected from around the world.

While chefs in other lands have taught their American counterparts much that is exciting and creative about the use of seasonings, let us note a point that is all too often overlooked. Indian cooking has a reputation for the skillful use of certain spices, French a genius for the use of herbs, Greek and Italian for other seasoning innovations. Yet these and other countries around the globe are really quite narrow in their concept of seasoning.

Do we hear foundations shaking and a heavily accented roar of contempt? Indeed, remarks a foreign chorus, hasn't the rest of the world had to teach Americans everything they know about seasoning?

Yes, yes, a thousand times yes! Yet, if one really studies the culinary genius of other lands, one discovers that the inspiration, albeit considerable, is in every case limited to certain tradition-bound tastes and techniques.

It has been our observation that Italians will not often cook Polish specialties, nor Frenchmen experiment much with Mexican dishes, nor Greeks with Polynesian. Most countries seem quite content with their own tastes, their own traditions.

But the United States? Because we are so truly a melting pot, serious cooks among us are gradually becoming the most adventurous, the most comprehensively skilled seasoners in the world. We are not tradition-bound. We freely borrow a dish from anywhere so long as it pleases the palate. We consider the culinary variations from around the world to be exciting adventures in taste. The thousands of ethnic restaurants sprinkled across our land have, in this regard, served as inspiring teachers. And each, hewing to its own tradition, has a vital role to play in pleasing the increasingly sophisticated palates of Americans.

But when all of the world's specialists have taught us their tricks, the professional chefs in this country will have the most exciting repertoire of recipes in the world, the most finesse with seasonings. It's an exciting concept of American cookery and one that contrasts markedly with the traditional image of "meat and potatoes" America.

In this text we have tried to look at the world of seasoning from the professional chef's perspective—to provide a ready reference to the many products which are apt to be on the professional's seasoning shelf, to explain, define, and contribute fresh information on products which are not now part of the chef's repertoire, but should be. In doing so, we hope that we have made our contribution to the seasoning of America.

Glossary of Seasonings

How much does a chef need to know about the seasonings he or she uses? From a strictly practical standpoint, one needs to know very little beyond what seasonings look like, what they smell like, and what effect they have on the foods in which they are used. But it is interesting and rewarding to know something about the nature and history of the seasonings we use. What do they consist of? Where do they come from? Traditionally, how have they been used? This kind of information makes cooking a fascinating and absorbing subject instead of a dull chore.

The glossary is designed to provide a quick and handy reference to the major seasonings and their uses; it will also serve as an introduction to their derivation. The information it contains will be sufficient to meet the needs of most good cooks. For those who might be interested in more serious study of this fascinating subject, a list of additional readings has been provided, beginning on page 268.

For some product categories (cheese, cordials and liqueurs, wines, dehydrated onion and garlic, flavoring extracts), information has been put into chart form. We have done this for several reasons. With extracts, for instance, the descriptive and source information would have been repetitious. With cheese and wine, it seemed more helpful for the chef to see the entire category at a glance. In the case of dehydrated onion and garlic, the numerous forms these ingredients can take were better illustrated in a chart. In all cases, however, the ingredients in the charts are also listed in the glossary for easy reference.

ACHIOTE (ANNATTO) SEEDS

The aromatic seed of a tropical tree that grows in Guyana and other parts of South America. Crush ½ teaspoon of seeds, and heat in one cup of lard for five minutes to make "sofrita," a reddish orange cooking sauce much used in Puerto Rican and Latin American dishes.

ALLSPICE

Small, dark brown berry of a tropical tree that flourishes in Jamaica, Guatemala, Honduras, and Mexico. The flavor tastes predominently like clove, but is milder, sweeter, and more mellow. The name allspice came about because people felt there were hints of cinnamon and nutmeg in the flavor, as well as clove. Use ground in baked goods, fruit desserts, yellow vegetables. Whole berries are used in stews, soups, and pickling liquids.

ALMOND EXTRACT

See Flavoring Extracts Chart.

ALMOND PASTE

Consists of blanched, finely ground almonds that are moistened and usually sweetened. Used in the filling of Danish pastry; for macaroons, marzipan candy and cakes, and other desserts.

ALMOND-TYPE CORDIALS

See Cordials/Liqueurs Seasoning Chart.

ANCHOVY PASTE

Consists of ground, prepared anchovy fillets. The product sold through foodservice supply channels usually contains additional seasonings. Used in sauces (particularly butter sauce for fish or steak), for canapés, and in Caesar and green goddess salad dressings.

ANISE SEEDS

Dried fruit (grayish brown seeds) of a small annual belonging to the parsley family; unmistakably identified by a strong licorice flavor. Sources are Spain, Egypt, Mexico, and Turkey. Whole seeds are most readily available. Whole seeds can be ground by hand. Used in baked goods, especially cookies and fruit pies, and in sweet fruit relishes.

APPLE PIE SPICE

A ground blend of sweet baking spices with a predominance of cinnamon, available as a commercial preparation. Cloves, nutmeg, or mace, allspice, and ginger are most typical of the other spices used. Good for all fruit pies and pastries.

APRICOT BRANDY

See Cordials/Liqueurs Seasoning Chart.

APRICOT EXTRACT

See Flavoring Extracts Chart.

AROMATIC BITTERS

This is a generic term for commercial concoctions like Angostura Bitters and several other brands. These are preparations made from ingredients such as spices, orange and lemon rinds, crushed prunes, gentian root, quassia chips, aloes, quinine, and rum. Used in old-fashioneds and other cocktails, bitters also give a delicious touch of

contrast to otherwise sweet fruit dishes, sauces, and glazes. Cream soups, sauces, and cheese canapés are enhanced by a few drops.

BANANA EXTRACT

See Flavoring Extracts Chart.

BARBECUE SPICE or SEASONING

Preparation made from paprika and other spices such as chili powder, garlic, and cloves, combined with salt and sugar. The basic seasoning for a barbecue sauce; good also in salad dressings, meat casseroles, hash browned potatoes, eggs and cheese dishes.

BASIL

Leaves of an annual herb belonging to the mint family, available fresh and dried. Packaged, dried basil leaves are bits of green leaves that are aromatic and mildly pungent. Grown in the United States, Hungary, France, and Bulgaria. Use in spaghetti sauce, cooked vegetables (especially tomatoes), seafood, poultry, and salads.

BAY LEAVES

Whole, large, fragrant, pale green leaves with slightly bitter taste. Mostly imported from Turkey. Bay leaves are sometimes referred to as "laurel," because they come from a laurel tree (Laurus nobilis). One or two leaves give excellent flavor to meats, potatoes, stews, soups, sauces, and fish.

BEEF EXTRACT

Any of a number of commercial products, in liquid or paste form, based on an extract of beef flavor. Often containing additional seasonings and artificial coloring. Used to enrich sauces, soups, and casseroles with meat flavor. Tends to be salty, so less table salt is needed when this product is used.

BEER

This common beverage is used as a seasoning in recipes like the famous Belgian Stew Beef Carbonnade and in batters for fish and seafood. There is, of course, a wide variety of beers available ranging from very dark and heavy to very light.

BELL PEPPERS

See SWEET PEPPER FLAKES.

BLACK WALNUT EXTRACT

See Flavoring Extracts Chart.

BLACKBERRY EXTRACT

See Flavoring Extracts Chart.

BLUE CHEESE

See Cheese Seasoning Chart.

BLUEBERRY EXTRACT

See Flavoring Extracts Chart.

BOUQUET GARNI

A bunch of herbs, principally bay leaves, thyme, and parsley, but may include others. Used to season stews, soups, and sauces. The blend is also available as a dried spice product in some brand lines.

BOURBON

The confection "bourbon balls" begins a long list of culinary specialties in which bourbon can play an important flavoring or seasoning role. Fruit glazes for poultry and pork, barbecue sauces, flambéed desserts, seafood sauces and stuffings, sautéed mushrooms, and other vegetable preparations are all made distinctive by a touch of bourbon.

BRANDY or COGNAC

Unless otherwise indicated in the name, brandy is derived from distilled grapes. It is often artificially colored and contains 40 to 60 percent alcohol. Brandy from the Charente region of France may be labeled cognac. Apples, blackberry, plums, oranges (Grand Marnier), and cherries are other popular fruits distilled to make brandy. Brandies are primarily used in cooking as flavoring for baked goods and dessert sauces, but they are also good in creamed sauces for seafood and poultry and in omelets and cheese dishes.

BRANDY EXTRACT

See Flavoring Extracts Chart.

BROWN or YELLOW BEAN SAUCE

Called *mien see* in Chinese, this thick, canned sauce is prepared from mashed soy beans, flour, and water. Much used as a seasoning in Chinese dishes, it imparts a flavor somewhat like that of soy sauce and can also be used as soy sauce would be in non-Chinese cooking. Once can is opened, sauce should be transferred to a glass container and refrigerated.

BURGUNDY (and other red table wines)

See Wines Seasoning Chart.

BUTTER

As used in numerous recipes, butter can most definitely be called a seasoning. For purest butter flavor, it should be clarified (heat until it foams and then skim the foam off). Browned butter gives still another seasoning effect. The amount of butter used, together with the amounts and kinds of other seasonings in a recipe, will determine whether the butter is a seasoning or a main ingredient. Hollandaise sauce exemplifies the use of butter as a seasoning; in most baking, butter acts as a main ingredient.

BUTTER PECAN EXTRACT

See Flavoring Extracts Chart.

CAPERS

Used as a condiment since ancient times, capers are the flower buds of a Mediterranean shrub, salted and packed in vinegar. Use in fish and chicken dishes, salads and sauces, with spinach or any vegetable that will benefit from a pleasing tartness. An essential ingredient in Gribiche Sauce; Caper Sauce for lamb, salmon, and white fish; Cambridge Sauce for mutton.

CARAWAY LIQUEUR

See Cordials/Liqueurs Seasoning Chart.

CARAWAY SEEDS

Sold whole. This curved brown seed from a plant belonging to the parsley family has a spicy, tangy taste. Imported from Netherlands, Poland, and Denmark. Use in rye bread and other baked goods, cheese dips and spreads, in pork and sauerkraut, and in beef casseroles.

CARDAMOM SEEDS

Sold as whole pods, seeds, or in ground form. Pods are naturally green, but are often blanched to white or straw color before they are sold. Seeds are almost black. They have a strong, exotic aroma and are popular in Scandinavian and Middle Eastern dishes. They are also used in coffee cakes, cookies, buns, pumpkin and apple pies, and in hot coffee. (This last use is a Middle Eastern custom, and the greatest percentage of cardamom worldwide is consumed in this way.) Imported from Guatemala and India.

CARROTS

One of the essential ingredients in the onion-carrot-celery mixture called *mirepoix* in which the vegetables are cooked into an essence for flavoring soups, stews, and sauces. Carrots add aroma as well as sweetness to a dish. As a rule, the redder the carrot, the finer the flavor.

CATSUP

A condiment consisting of a thick, smooth-textured, spicy sauce usually made with tomatoes, although there are mushroom, walnut, and other catsups as well. Essentially a pour-on sauce for meats, fish cakes, eggs, and beans, but also a flavoring ingredient in some casseroles, sauces, dips, and wherever sweetened tomato flavor is desired.

CAYENNE

See RED PEPPER.

CELERY

This familiar vegetable is primarily used as a seasoning in sauces, soups, and stews. The leaves have the strongest flavor.

CELERY FLAKES

Dehydrated and flaked vegetable celery ribs and leaves. Useful in any dish where celery flavor is desired, such as stuffings, sauces, and stews.

CELERY SALT

Ground celery seeds combined with table salt. This is a sprinkle-on seasoning for fish, seafood, and salads. Also good in tomato juice and as a garnish for Bloody Marys.

CELERY SEEDS

From an herb known as smallage or wild celery grown primarily in India—related to, but distinct from domestically grown vegetable celery. The tiny, brown, pungent seeds are used in sauces, salads such as cole slaw, dips, and fish and seafood dishes.

CHABLIS or SAUTERNE and other white table wines

See Wines Seasoning Chart.

CHAMPAGNE (and other sparkling wines)

See Wines Seasoning Chart.

CHEDDAR CHEESE

See Cheese Seasoning Chart.

CHERRY EXTRACT

See Flavoring Extracts Chart.

CHERRY-TYPE-LIQUEURS

See Cordials/Liqueurs Seasoning Chart.

CHERVIL

The leaves of an annual herb belonging to the parsley family. In its dried form, chervil is usually sold as "whole leaves" which are actually broken bits. Grown in France and the United States. This herb can be used as an alternative to parsley, but has more aroma and faintly suggests tarragon. Especially popular in French dishes, salads, stuffings, sauces, and omelets.

CHILI POWDER

A blend of ground chili peppers, garlic powder, oregano, ground cumin seed, and a little salt. May contain red pepper for more spiciness. Color varies from bright red to mahogany. The darker type has been toasted to caramelize the natural sugars of the chili peppers.) This powder is the principal seasoning for chili con carne, but it is also a delicious seasoning variation for just about any other meat, poultry, or fish dish, or for soups, salads, and dips.

CHILLIES (See also RED PEPPER).

This is a general term for small, hot red peppers of various types (e.g. chili pequins, birdseye peppers, tabasco peppers). In the spice trade, "chillies" are distinct from "chili peppers." The latter are much larger and milder and are used primarily in chili powder.

CHINESE FIVE SPICES

A blend of black pepper, cloves, cinnamon, fennel, and star anise used for seasoning chicken, duck, and pork. If not available commercially, mix in blender 2 tablespoons black peppercorns, 36 whole cloves, 12 inches of stick cinnamon, 2 tablespoons fennel seed, and 12 whole star anise fruit.

CHINESE PARSLEY

See CILANTRO.

CHIVES

Now available fresh, frozen, or in freeze-dried form. The slender, tubular chive shoots have a delicate onion flavor. Grown in the United States. Use with sour cream for baked potatoes, eggs, cottage cheese, cooked vegetables, creamy sauces, yogurt, and creamed soups. They are especially good in vichyssoise.

CHOCOLATE AND COCOA

Both of these flavors begin with the cacao bean. This bean comes from the Theobroma tree which flourishes in tropical America. To make chocolate, the beans are milled to a liquor; when cooled this liquor becomes the unsweetened chocolate used for baking. Milk and sugar plus extra cocoa butter are added to the liquor to produce milk chocolate. Cocoa is made from liquor that has part of the cocoa butter removed. Dutch chocolate is made by treating the ground cacao beans with certain alkalis to darken the color.

CILANTRO (See also CORIANDER).

This is the Spanish term for the leaves of the coriander plant. It is also known as Chinese parsley. Used in many Latin American, Russian, and East European stews, casseroles, sauces, and salads, cilantro grows in Argentina, Mexico, Morocco, as well as parts of Europe and the U.S.

CINNAMON and CASSIA

Bark from any of several trees belonging to the cinnamomum family can be labeled cinnamon. Most of the cinnamon the United States imports is Cinnamomum cassia; hence those in the spice trade often use the term "cassia" to refer to cinnamon. Cassia-type cinnamon is the familiar reddish brown color; it has a strong flavor and comes from Indonesia and China. Cinnamon from Ceylon is pale tan in comparison and mild in flavor with a sweet undertone. Most of our import from Ceylon is transshipped to Mexico; almost none is used in the U.S. While cinnamon is best known as our favorite baking spice, try it also with meats—in stews particularly—as well as with fruit and in coffee and cocoa.

CINNAMON SUGAR

Sugar that is blended with ground cinnamon. A quick topping for cinnamon toast and other sweet baked goods.

CLOVES

This nail-shaped flower bud has a very strong, sweet aroma. It is available whole or in ground form. Imported from Madagascar, Zanzibar, and Indonesia. Use whole cloves in baked ham, fruit syrups, pickling vinegars, and stews. Ground cloves are used in baked goods, other desserts, and beverages. Be respectful of its potency!

COCONUT

Flaked or desiccated coconut, coconut milk, and coconut cream are all available as flavor adjuncts today. Principal uses are in baking, but the various forms of coconut are also used as seasoning in curries and other East Indian and Oriental main dishes as well as in beverages.

COCONUT EXTRACT

See Flavoring Extracts Chart.

COFFEE

When used as a flavoring ingredient, coffee is usually brewed first. The effect it has in a recipe is a function of the strength of the brew as well as the type of bean chosen. Coffee is much used in frostings, cakes, and fillings.

COFFEE-TYPE LIQUEURS

See Cordials/Liqueurs Seasoning Chart.

COINTREAU EXTRACT

See Flavoring Extracts Chart.

COON CHEESE

See Cheese Seasoning Chart.

CORIANDER SEEDS

Available whole or ground, these small seeds from an herb belonging to the parsley family have a mild, lemony flavor. Imported from Mexico, Morocco, and Argentina. Coriander is always included in curry powder and mixed pickling spice and is often used as a meat seasoning in Middle Eastern cookery. Try it also as a flavoring in buns, pastry, cookies, and cake.

CRAB BOIL or SHRIMP SPICE

This is a mixture of whole peppercorns, bay leaves, red peppers, mustard seeds, ginger root, and other spices. Add a few tablespoons to the water when boiling seafood to add hot flavor and aroma.

CUMIN SEEDS

Available whole or ground, this is a yellowish brown seed with a strong aroma reminiscent of caraway. Imported from Iran and India. It is used in chili and curry powders and in deviled eggs, sauerkraut, and sauerkraut dishes. Also good in rice, pork, and cheese dishes. Though it is already in commercially prepared chili powder, many cooks add extra cumin to develop more of the aromatic flavor characteristic of chili con carne.

CURRY POWDER

A spice blend typically containing such spices as ground coriander, cumin, fenugreek, red pepper, turmeric, allspice, cassia, cardamom, cloves, fennel, ginger, mace, mustard, and black or white pepper. In addition to curries, it makes an interesting seasoning variation for eggs, vegetables, soups, salad dressings, and dips.

DEHYDRATED GARLIC

See Dehydrated Onion and Dehydrated Garlic Charts.

DEHYDRATED ONION

See Dehydrated Onion and Dehydrated Garlic Charts.

DILL SEEDS

These light brown, oval seeds with a spicy, carawaylike taste are most readily available as whole seeds. Primarily imported from India. Use in pickles, fish, sauces, cabbage, green beans, salad dressings, and sour cream soups.

DILL WEED

Refers to the dried leaves of the dill plant. Like fresh dill, the flavor of the leaves suggests a combination of fennel and mint. Used in sauces for fish and seafood (especially Scandinavian recipes), salads, vegetables, and dips. Produced in the United States.

ECHALOTE or ESCHALOTS

See SHALLOTS.

FAGARA

See SZECHUAN PEPPER.

FENNEL SEEDS

Available whole, these are the yellowish brown seeds of an herb of the parsley family and have an aroma like licorice. Imported from India, Lebanon, China. Use on breads, rolls, coffee cakes, in chicken and seafood sauces, and in pork dishes. Also good with sweet yellow vegetables.

FENUGREEK SEEDS

The seed of a plant belonging to the pea family, it has a pleasantly bitter flavor and a currylike aroma. Supplied by Morocco, Egypt, and India. Fenugreek can be obtained but is not readily available.

Principal use to the chef would be in the preparation of homemade curry powder.

FILE POWDER (also called GUMBO FILE)

Dried leaves of the Sassafras tree. Some prepared products also contain thyme or other herbs. From the United States. Used in gumbo and other Creole dishes as a thickening agent and for its bitter, aromatic flavor.

FINES HERBES

A combination of three or more dried herbs. Typical ingredients include parsley, chervil, tarragon, savory, thyme, marjoram, and sage. Available ready-made in some spice lines. Used in omelets, sauces, and salads.

FONTINA CHEESE

See Cheese Seasoning Chart.

FREEZE-DRIED CHIVES

See Dehydrated Onion and Dehydrated Garlic Charts.

FREEZE-DRIED SHALLOTS

See Dehydrated Onion and Dehydrated Garlic Charts.

GARLIC

Fresh garlic is a cured bulb composed of "cloves." The joined cloves are encased in a tissue-thin white skin, and the whole bulb is called a "head." From the United States. Use with all kinds of meats, shellfish, bread, salad dressings, soups, sauces, and casseroles.

GINGER

An irregularly shaped, dried root with a spicy, hot flavor. Available either whole or ground in the dried form and as fresh, whole roots. Imported from Jamaica, India, Nigeria, China, and Australia. Use ground in gingerbread, spice cakes, marinades, and sauces. Whole roots can be used in pickling liquids and fruit syrups. A whole, dried root soaked in water for several hours may be sliced or grated as would be done with a fresh root. Both reconstituted dried roots and fresh roots are important in Far Eastern cookery, especially in main dishes and sauces.

GORGONZOLA CHEESE

See Cheese Seasoning Chart.

GRAINS OF PARADISE

Small, dark brown aromatic seeds from a plant in the ginger family, native to the African Gold Coast. Used in place of pepper in foods of West African origin.

GRENADINE

A sweet syrup made from pomegranates used in beverages and desserts. Sometimes contains alcohol. A sprinkling over grapefruit halves is a classic use, and it is also delicious as a basting sauce for chicken.

GUMBO FILE POWDER

See FILE POWDER.

HERB SEASONING

A savory blend of herbs such as marjoram, oregano, basil, and chervil combined with salt. Especially flavorful in salads and salad dressings, but also good in omelets, hamburgers, and casseroles.

HOISIN SAUCE

A reddish brown, sweet sauce made of soy beans, flour, sugar, spices, water, and garlic. It may also contain chili peppers. Like bean sauce, it is an important seasoning in Chinese cooking and can also be used for interestingly different flavor effects in sauces for non-Chinese dishes. Try it with pork, beef, and chicken sauces.

HONEY

There are some 300 kinds of honey sold in the United States, but the most common—from clover—is usually the one chosen for cooking purposes. It can be used with, or in place of, sugar. If you are substituting honey for sugar in a baking recipe, less honey will be needed, depending on the thickness of the honey and the amount of sugar being replaced, since honey is sweeter than a comparable amount of sugar.

HORSERADISH

This root of a wild herb has a hot, penetrating pungence which adds a deliciously piquant note to sauces and dressings for meats, fish, salads, and vegetables. Fresh horseradish can be prepared by grating the root but must be used immediately as it is very perishable. Various prepared horseradish sauces that store well in the refrigerator are also used for seasoning. For a horseradish flavor, horseradish powder is readily available today and may be stored at room temperature.

HOT OIL

Much used in Chinese cooking, this is simply vegetable oil (such as peanut or sesame) in which hot red peppers have been heated to create a spicy infusion. It gives any foods fried in it a spicy character. Commercially available in Chinese groceries, it is also easily prepared in the kitchen by adding 1 oz. ground red pepper to a cup of oil.

ITALIAN SEASONING

A blend of ground herbs—oregano, basil and rosemary—red pepper and sometimes garlic powder. Used in spaghetti sauces, salad dressings, pizza toppings, tomato, zucchini and green bean dishes, cheese souffles, and stuffings.

JAPANESE PEPPER

See SZECHUAN PEPPER.

JUNIPER BERRIES

Bluish gray, berrylike fruit of the juniper tree. They are especially popular in Scandinavian and German cooking, in marinades, sauerkraut, and game dishes. Juniper is an important flavoring for gin. It will also enhance duck, lamb, ham, or beef stew.

KETCHUP

See CATSUP.

LEEK

A plant related to the onion with a white, slender bulb and dark green leaves. Leek flavor is similar to that of onion but milder and sweeter. Use thinly sliced as a seasoning in salads, soups, stews, and sauces.

LEMON EXTRACT

See Flavoring Extracts Chart.

LEMON JUICE

Of all the citrus fruits, lemons are the most used as a seasoning. The tart juice has the property of accenting other flavors much the same way salt does. Fresh and bottled juices are widely used as seasonings for sauces, salad dressings, marinades, and desserts.

LEMON PEEL

The peel or rind of the lemon has the most concentrated flavor of the fruit and is much used in baking as well as in sauces and desserts. When fresh lemons are used, the peel is grated for flavoring, but only the outer yellow portion—the zest—should be used; the white can be bitter. Also available is a dehydrated, grated lemon peel or rind.

LIME EXTRACT

See Flavoring Extracts Chart.

LIME JUICE

This is the second most popular seasoning among the citrus fruits. It is particularly good with fish, seafood, and other fruits like melons. Juice is the principal part of the lime used and is available bottled as well as fresh.

LIQUID HOT PEPPER SAUCE

This is the generic term for Tabasco sauce and a number of other similar brand name products. It is essentially an extraction of heat and flavor from small, fiery red peppers in a liquid medium, usually vinegar.

Other seasonings may be present. Strength varies considerably according to brand. Price is usually a clue with the higher priced brands stronger than the less expensive ones. In using, remember that you can always add more, but you can't subtract. A little of this sauce can bring new flavor interest to sauces, soups, salad dressings, and casserole dishes.

MACE

See NUTMEG.

MAPLE EXTRACT

See Flavoring Extracts Chart.

MAPLE SYRUP

Use whenever the quality of maple flavor is critical. For flavoring purposes in recipes, pancake syrups are often substituted, but the flavor is not the same as true maple syrup.

MAPLE WALNUT EXTRACT

See Flavoring Extracts Chart.

MARJORAM

Whole or ground leaves of an herb belonging to the mint family. The whole, dried form consists of bits of grayish green leaves with aromatic, savory flavor. Imported from France and Egypt. Use with roast meats, poultry, fish, green vegetables, salads, and herbed breads.

MARSALA

See Wines Seasoning Chart.

MINT

Available fresh in sprigs or as dehydrated flakes of spearmint or peppermint leaves. Both spearmint and peppermint have a strong, sweet aroma and a cool aftertaste; however the two flavors are also distinctively different. Peppermint is more biting, spearmint more seemingly sweet. From Egypt, Bulgaria, and the United States. Popular in candies, frozen desserts, chocolate, fruits, tossed green salads, carrots, and peas. Mint jelly and mint sauce are classic accompaniments to roast lamb.

MIREPOIX

See CARROTS.

MIXED PICKLING SPICE

One of the oldest blends, it includes whole spices such as mustard seed, bay leaves, black and white peppercorns, dill seed, red peppers, ginger, cinnamon, mace, allspice, and coriander seed. Used in pickling, cooked marinades, soups, stews, and sauces.

MIXED VEGETABLE FLAKES

A mixture of dehydrated, flaked vegetables, usually including onions, celery, green and red peppers, and carrots. A convenient seasoning for soups, stews, sauces, and stuffings. To reconstitute, add an equal amount of water and let stand 10 minutes.

MOLASSES

Once our primary sweetener, molasses today is used more as a flavoring in baked goods, frostings, candies, sauces, puddings, and other desserts. Industrial users can now get molasses in a dry form, but the familiar viscous liquid is still the standard form available through foodservice supply channels.

MONOSODIUM GLUTAMATE

A white, crystalline compound. Colorless and tasteless itself, it stimulates the taste buds to emphasize the natural flavors of vegetable, soup, seafood, meat, or poultry. Use sparingly: a half teaspoon is enough for six portions of food.

MONTEREY JACK CHEESE

See Cheese Seasoning Chart.

MUSCATEL

See Wines Seasoning Chart.

MUSHROOM POWDER

Dehydrated, powdered mushrooms. Specifically for use as a seasoning whenever mushroom flavor is appropriate but texture is not required. Can be used along with fresh or canned mushrooms to intensify flavor.

MUSTARD SEED

Available whole, ground or powdered. (The powdered form is often referred to as "mustard flour.") Tiny seeds, yellowish to reddish brown. Whole seed is used primarily in pickling and in mixed pickling spice. The ground form is mainly used by the sausage industry. Powder (or "flour") is the more common culinary ingredient. It is a flour, because the hull has been removed. Unique among spices, it does not develop flavor until triggered by liquid. Mix with an equal amount of water at room temperature and allow 10 minutes for flavor to develop. From Canada, the United Kingdom, Denmark and the United States. Use in meat, fish, fowl dishes, in sauces and salad dressings, in cheese and egg dishes.

MUSTARD, PREPARED

A condiment consisting of mustard flour in vinegar with spices, sugar, and thickening agents that vary according to the type of mustard. The yellower products are colored with turmeric. Numerous uses in flavoring, particularly in sauces, dressings, and various casseroles.

NIGELLA SEEDS or RUSSIAN BLACK CARAWAY

Look like small pieces of burnt charcoal. Has a heavily perfumed aroma, and the flavor is mild and somewhat peppery. Used mainly by Slavic people on rye and egg loaf bread. It is available in localities with a heavy Slavic or Middle Eastern heritage.

NUTMEG and MACE

Both come from the peachlike fruit of an evergreen tree. The aroma of nutmeg is sweeter and more delicate than mace, while mace is more positive in its flavor. Either spice comes in ground or whole form, but whole mace ("blades") is not as readily available as whole nutmeg. Imported from Indonesia and the West Indies. Use nutmeg not only in baked goods and desserts, but in chicken soup, corn custard, spinach, and candied sweet potatoes. Mace is especially good in pound cake, cherry pie, and fish sauces.

OLIVE OIL

Since this oil, in contrast to many cooking oils, contributes such a distinctive flavor, it must be considered a seasoning. Flavor varies quite a bit according to brand and that, in turn, varies according to place of origin and kind of processing. The flavor ranges from heavy and strong to light and fruity. Salads, appetizers, vegetables, and meat dishes are all enhanced by olive oil. Spain and Italy are our main sources today.

ONIONS

The following types of fresh onions are available almost all year: *Medium yellow:* Strong aroma; for chopping, stuffing. *Large yellow:* Somewhat milder than medium yellow, all-purpose, excellent for stuffing, slicing. *Large Bermuda or Spanish:* Comparatively mild, fine for slicing and French-frying. *Small white:* Mild, often used as a vegetable rather than a seasoning. *Red:* Smaller ones are more pungent than larger. Used in salads, as garnishes.

ORANGE EXTRACT

See Flavoring Extracts Chart.

ORANGE JUICE

Not as universally used as lemon juice for seasoning, orange juice is still very popular as a flavoring for baked goods and other desserts and in sauces, especially those for seafood and poultry.

ORANGE PEEL

Can either be grated from a fresh orange or purchased as a dehydrated, powdered product. As with lemon peel, only the outer surface should be used; the white portion can be bitter. Because of its concentrated flavor, it is widely used in baking, dessert making, and in sauces—whenever a strong orange flavor is desired.

ORANGE-TYPE LIQUEURS

See Liqueurs/Cordials Seasoning Chart.

OREGANO

Available dried as a whole leaf or in ground form. Packaged oregano consists of small pieces of green leaves with strong, pleasant aroma and taste. Imported from the Mediterranean area and Mexico. Known as the "pizza herb," it is also excellent in spaghetti sauces, meat, cheese, fish, and egg dishes. The Mediterranean type is the best choice for Italian and Greek cooking, while the Mexican variety is best suited to chili con carne and other Mexican dishes.

PAPRIKA

Available ground only. A rich red powder with a slightly sweet taste, although some types have varying degrees of bite. From the United States, Spain, and Hungary. (Nippier paprika is available from Hungary where they often use this spice as a flavoring, but Hungary also ships sweet paprika today.) Use sweet paprika as "the garnish spice." Also good for mild flavor in creamed, bland foods such as Welsh rarebit, deviled eggs, sour creamed dips, and bisques.

PARISIENNE SPICE or QUATRE EPICES

A blend of spices, popular in France, for marinades, pea soup, stews, sweet yellow vegetables. It is hard to find ready-mixed, but one formula can be prepared by mixing 5 tablespoons ground cloves, 3 tablespoons ground white pepper, 3 teaspoons ground nutmeg, and 3 teaspoons ground ginger. Its flavor can also be roughly simulated by using a blend of half ground allspice and half ground white pepper.

PARMESAN CHEESE

See Cheese Seasoning Chart.

PARSLEY

It comes fresh as curly parsley, the familiar variety used as garnish and seasoning, and Italian parsley. The latter type has a plain, flat leaf, is very dark in color and has a rich flavor. (So-called "Chinese parsley" is really cilantro or coriander leaves.)

PARSLEY FLAKES

Flakes of dried, bright green parsley leaves with mild, agreeable aroma and taste. From the United States and Hungary. Use in sauces for meats, poultry, fish, vegetables, scrambled eggs, stuffings and soups.

PEACH EXTRACT

See Flavoring Extracts Chart.

PEPPER, BLACK

"The master spice." Available as whole peppercorns, ground, coarse ground, or cracked. (The coarser grinds may also be labeled butcher's grind, gourmet grind, peppermill grind.) A single berry is the source of either black or white pepper. For black pepper, the berry is picked while slightly underripe and dried. The whole berry is used. For white pepper, the dark outer hull is removed and only the light-colored kernel is used. Imported from Indonesia, India, and Brazil. Used with all kinds of meats, vegetables, salads. A pinch of ground black pepper is delicious in spice cakes and cookies.

PEPPER, WHITE

Available whole or ground. Light-colored kernel of a ripe peppercorn. Less aromatic than black pepper, but still pungent. Use it in pale sauces and mayonnaise where black specks would otherwise show.

PEPPERCORNS, GREEN

Soft, immature pepper berries which are bottled with wine vinegar or brine. Primarily from Madagascar. Quite pungent, but somewhat milder than dried black pepper. Use crushed or mashed in pepper sauces and dips or spread over meat or chicken before broiling. A freeze-dried version has also been developed.

PEPPERMINT EXTRACT

See Flavoring Extracts Chart.

PINEAPPLE EXTRACT

See Flavoring Extracts Chart.

PISTACHIO EXTRACT

See Flavoring Extracts Chart.

POPPY SEEDS

Available whole only. A tiny, slate blue seed with a rich nutlike taste, from a plant known as *Papaver somniferum.* Imported from the Netherlands, Turkey, and Romania. Use as topping for rolls, breads, and cookies and in cole slaw, noodles, dips, and cheesecake. Crushed poppy seeds (easily done in a blender) make delicious pastry fillings when mixed with honey.

PORT

See Wines Seasoning Chart.

POULTRY SEASONING

A ground blend consisting of sage, thyme, marjoram, and savory and sometimes rosemary and other spices. For poultry, veal, pork, and fish stuffings and coatings.

PUMPKIN PIE SPICE

A ground blend of cinnamon, nutmeg, cloves, and ginger. Designed especially for pumpkin pie, it is good also in spice cakes and cookies, gingerbread, and coffee cake. Excellent on sweet, yellow vegetables.

QUATRE EPICES

See PARISIENNE SPICE.

RASPBERRY EXTRACT

See Flavoring Extracts Chart.

RED PEPPER

Those in the spice trade have begun using the term red pepper to mean *any* product made from dried, hot red peppers. Available as whole peppers (chillies), crushed, and ground. The term cayenne had for a long time meant the hottest ground red pepper, but cayenne is now being phased out, because it has no standard heat measurement. Industrial buyers can specify the level of hotness they want in red pepper. Foodservice buyers are usually offered only one level, ground red pepper, but this is extremely hot and adequate to any cooking needs. The little red peppers which go into this product come from many countries, with China, Mexico, Pakistan, and India prominent. Crushed red pepper has the same bite as ground red, but the particles are larger. Ground red pepper is used in dips, sauces, soups, meats, fish. Crushed is used in heroes, pizza, spaghetti sauce, and Mexican dishes. Whole pods are used in pickles and marinades.

REGGIANO CHEESE

See Cheese Seasoning Chart.

ROMANO CHEESE

See Cheese Seasoning Chart.

ROQUEFORT CHEESE

See Cheese Seasoning Chart.

ROSE

See Wines Seasoning Chart.

ROSEMARY

This herb is available in dried form as whole rosemary which is actually bits of needlelike green leaves. It has a bittersweet taste. Imported from Portugal, France, and Yugoslavia. Excellent with lamb, chicken, beef, or pork; sauces for fish; salad dressings; eggplants, green beans, summer squashes, and mushrooms.

RUM

This distilled mash of sugar cane or molasses has many seasoning uses in cooking. Some uses are: basting sauces for meat, in marinades, quiches, dips, casseroles, cakes, pies, fruit desserts, and beverages.

RUM EXTRACT

See Flavoring Extracts Chart.

SAFFRON

Known as the world's most expensive spice, saffron is available whole or ground. Orange yellow flower stigmas with a pleasantly bitter taste and a potent coloring effect. Mostly imported from Spain. The price is so high, because it takes 225,000 stigmas, which must be hand-picked, to make a pound. Essential in Spanish cooking and much used in other Latin countries. Excellent with rice, seafood, and poultry.

SAGE

Dried sage is available whole as a leaf; ground, and rubbed (crumbled rather than ground, creating a fluffy texture). Long, grayish green leaves with strong, slightly bitter taste. Imported from Yugoslavia, Albania, Turkey. Use in sausage and poultry stuffings, meat loaves, pork dishes, fish chowders, and melted cheese dishes.

SALT

This familiar mineral product functions almost entirely as a seasoning. Coarse, Kosher, or pickling salt produces a more pronounced flavor than common table salt. Salt has the property of bringing out or emphasizing other flavors, particularly the savory spices. This quality is sometimes overlooked. If the amount of salt is reduced in a recipe, it will be necessary to increase the amount of herb in the dish.

SAUTERNE

See Wines Seasoning Chart.

SAVORY

Dried savory is available whole or ground. As packaged, the whole leaf product is really bits of greenish brown leaves with somewhat minty aroma. Imported from Yugoslavia, France. Use on green beans, meat, chicken, dressings, scrambled eggs, omelets, soups, and salad dressings.

SEASONED or FLAVORED SALT

This product goes by different names according to brand, but generally is a mixture of spices, herbs, and salt designed to be an all-purpose seasoning. Use on meats, vegetables, sauces, and dairy foods. Many restaurants put it on the table with salt and pepper.

SESAME SEEDS

Whole, creamy white seed, high in oil content, with a mild and nutty taste. Imported from Central America and Ethiopia. Toasting brings out the flavor, hence it is important to toast before using in salads, sauces, dips, stuffings and, casseroles. When using as a topping for baked goods, the seeds may be added raw because they will toast in the baking process. Large users can have a choice of hulled and unhulled seeds. Hulled are used mostly in toppings and for rolls, unhulled in breads.

SHALLOTS

A member of the onion family, shallots ("échalote" in French) have a delicate flavor combining onion and garlic. Like garlic, they grow in "cloves." Louisiana is the biggest producer. Widely used in place of onion in French cooking, especially in chicken and veal dishes. Sometimes minced scallions are used as a substitute.

SHERRY

See Wines Seasoning Chart.

SHERRY EXTRACT

See Flavoring Extracts Chart.

SHRIMP SPICE

19 See CRAB BOIL.

SMOKE FLAVOR or CHARCOAL SEASONING

These products go by various names and may be either dry or liquid preparations. The base is wood smoke concentrate, often hickory, with salt and other ingredients that vary with the brand. These seasonings give a strong smoked flavor when brushed or sprinkled on meats before grilling. Other uses include in baked beans, pea soup, barbecue sauce, and egg dishes.

SOUR CREAM

Commercially, this is light cream to which a culture of lactic acid bacteria has been added. It has many flavoring uses, especially in Russian and Slavic dishes. Add at the last minute to sauces and hot mixtures and heat only until hot. Do not boil, since boiling may curdle sour cream.

SOUR SALT

This is a citric acid, a crystalline compound with an agreeably tart taste. It is often used to flavor foods and in the manufacture of carbonated beverages. It can be made from fresh fruit juices or synthetically.

SOY SAUCE

A lightly fermented liquid generally made of soybeans, wheat or barley flour, water, and salt. It is much used in Oriental cooking for flavor in place of salt. The liquid is usually dark brown in color, but color and flavor can vary due to different manufacturing processes. In addition to its use in Oriental recipes, soy sauce makes an excellent marinade and will give an exotic flavor touch to all types of meat, seafood, and vegetable dishes.

STAR ANISE

Handsome, star-shaped fruit of an evergreen tree with a pleasant aniselike taste and sweet, aniselike aroma. It is not related to the plant which gives us anise seed. Available whole only, it is used as a flavoring agent in confections and makes an eye-catching addition to stewed fruit and pickle recipes. Imported from China.

STEAK SAUCES

Though mostly used as pour-on products, these are sometimes also used as flavoring ingredients in recipes today. Formulas vary according to the manufacturer. A more viscous consistency, as well as the flavor, separates most steak sauces from products like Worcestershire and soy sauces.

STILTON CHEESE

See Cheese Seasoning Chart.

STRAWBERRY EXTRACT

See Flavoring Extracts Chart.

SWEET PEPPER FLAKES or BELL PEPPER FLAKES

Dehydrated, flaked sweet green or red peppers, or a mixture of both green and red (sweet red, not hot). Use in sauces, salads, vegetables, casseroles, or when finely diced pepper is needed. To soften, add an equal amount of water and let stand 10 minutes.

SZECHUAN PEPPER (also called FAGARA or JAPANESE PEPPER)

Peppercornlike fruits of a deciduous tree grown in south-central China. Moderately spicy, but primarily a spice which brings out the true flavor of other ingredients. Available in whole form. Widely used in Chinese and Japanese cooking. (Szechuan Chinese cooking is known to be quite pungent, but the spiciness comes primarily from red pepper, not Szechuan pepper.)

TANGERINE EXTRACT

See Flavoring Extracts Chart.

TARRAGON

Dried tarragon comes in leaf form. It is a perennial herb belonging to the aster family with an aroma which has a hint of anise about it. Imported from France and Yugoslavia. Famous in vinegars and salad dressings, seafood or egg salads, chicken or seafood dishes.

THYME

Whole or ground dried leaves of an herb belonging to the mint family. A favorite herb in American cooking for generations. Imported from Spain and France. Use it in Manhattan-style clam chowder, creole seafood, poultry stuffings, creamed chicken, and with green beans, eggplant, onions, and tomatoes.

TOKAY

See Wines Seasoning Chart.

TOMATO PASTE

When cooked and seasoned, tomato becomes an important flavoring. Tomato paste is a very thick concentrate made from cooked tomatoes and used as both a thickener and flavoring agent. Generally seasoned only with salt.

TOMATO PUREE

Like unseasoned paste. Strained, thick, but still liquid.

TOMATO SAUCE

Made from puréed tomatoes and seasoned with salt, pepper, and, generally, other spices and herbs such as basil and oregano. Most frequently used in making numerous other sauces, especially Italian-style.

TRUFFLES

A highly esteemed, very expensive variety of fleshy underground fungus used sparingly as a garnish and flavoring in paté de foie gras, sauces, omelets, and salads. Primarily an import, black truffles come from Perigord, France, while Piedmont, Italy, is famous for a cream-to-beige variety. Truffles must be discovered and uprooted by either specially trained dogs or pigs. They vary in size from that of a small marble to an orange.

TURMERIC

Aromatic root of a plant related to ginger. Not only has it an exotic aroma, but its saffron yellow color is so potent that it has been used as a dye. Always in ground form, it is one of the important spices in curry powder and is used in some mustards and mustard pickles. Imported from India. Use in chicken, seafood or egg dishes, or with rice, creamed potatoes, and macaroni.

VANILLA BEAN

Long, podlike seed capsule or fruit of a tropical orchid which, when suitably cured, browned, and dried, gives us the highly perfumed vanilla bean. The bean is lightly frosted with a crystalline essence which yields the flavor. One or two split beans buried in several pounds of sugar for a week or longer will become the classic vanilla sugar used in fancy desserts. Or, it can be steeped in hot milk and the milk then added as usual to baked goods, sweet fillings, and puddings.

VANILLA EXTRACT

See Flavoring Extracts Chart.

VERMOUTH

See Wines Seasoning Chart.

VINEGARS

The main types marketed in the United States today are distilled white; cider or apple cider; and distilled vinegar with apple cider flavoring (relatively new). Others commonly available include red or white wine, herbed, herbed wine, and malt. Innumerable dishes are enhanced by the right touch of tart vinegar, from sweet and sour ones to simply savory ones. Major uses of cider and white vinegars are in soups, sauces, dressings, and marinades; herbed and wine vinegars are good in all of these dishes and add another flavor dimension; malt vinegar is especially suited to fried fish.

WORCESTERSHIRE SAUCE

A commercial blend of vinegar, molasses, sugar, anchovies, soy sauce, tamarinds, onion, garlic, and spices. There are no standard proportions, so the blend varies according to brand. Originally a pour-on sauce, it is now used more as a seasoning in recipes according to the leading manufacturer. Essential in Bloody Marys, it is especially compatible with cheese and meat dishes and in salad dressings, sauces, and stews.

Seasoning Charts

CHEESE

Types	Seasoning Uses	Types	Seasoning Uses

BLUE-VEINED CHEESES
  Blue
  Gorgonzola
  Roquefort
  Stilton
	Salad dressings, sauces, for vegetables, poultry, beef, egg dishes, batters, stuffings, dips.	FONTINA
		
		PARMESAN-TYPE CHEESES
		  Parmesan
		  Reggiano
		  Romano
			Grating over pasta dishes, vegetables, veal, poultry.
			
			Grating over tomato-sauced dishes, vegetables, in dressings, bread crumb toppings, over soups, in casseroles.

CHEDDAR-TYPE CHEESES
  Cheddar
  Coon
  Monterey Jack
	Sauces, casseroles, toppings, fillings, souffles, cream soups, dips, rolls, breads.		

Note: The cheese chart and the wines chart that follows are meant not as comprehensive guides to the innumerable varieties of cheeses and wines. Rather they are intended to serve as handy references to the kinds of cheeses and wines most frequently used as seasonings and a guide to their uses as flavoring products.

CORDIALS and LIQUEURS

Types	Seasoning Uses
ALMOND (e.g. Amaretto, Noyaux)	With chocolate; in seasoning vegetables, pork, cherries.
APRICOT	In fruit compotes, cake and pastry fillings. Mix a little into apricot preserves for a delicious topping.
CARAWAY (e.g. Kummel)	Add to sauerkraut and boiled cabbage as well as other vegetables such as Brussels sprouts, broccoli, carrots, and cauliflower.
CHERRY (e.g. Kirschwasser, Cherry Heering)	Sauces for poultry; chocolate icings, toppings, whipped cream and custard fillings and toppings.
COFFEE (e.g. Tia Maria, Kahlua)	Add to shaved chocolate for vanilla ice cream topping; use in icings, fillings, with cherries, bananas, strawberries.
ORANGE (e.g. Grand Marnier, Curacao, Triple Sec, Cointreau)	As a glaze for ham or carrots; in sauces for poultry and fish; in barbecue bastings; with veal and pork.

WINES

Types	Seasoning Uses
BURGUNDY (or other dry red table wines)	Red meat stews, casseroles, sauces.
CHABLIS (or sauterne or other white table wines)	Fish, seafood sauces and stuffings, poultry, veal, pork.
CHAMPAGNE (or rose, cold duck, pink chablis or other sparkling wines)	Fruit cups and compotes, punches, sauces for poultry, fruit desserts.
MARSALA	Veal, poultry sauces and stuffings, most Italian-style dishes.
PORT (or tokay, muscatel, cream sherry, sweet vermouth, or other dessert wines)	Sauces for game, ham, poultry, and in desserts.
SHERRY (dry or cocktail type)	Creamed soups and sauces, stuffed mushrooms, meat, poultry, seafood casseroles.
VERMOUTH (dry or cocktail type)	Veal, pork, or poultry, cheese sauces, fish, seafood.

DEHYDRATED ONIONS

Types	Descriptions	Seasoning Uses
ONIONS:		
Powder	Fine powder, often contains food-grade calcium stearate for free flowing.	Hamburgers, salad dressings, vegetables. Rub into roasts, poultry, steaks, and chops. Use as last minute seasoning.
Granulated	Approximate consistency of granulated sugar; often contains calcium stearate for free flow.	Same as for powder, particularly when free flow is desirable.
Ground	Particles slightly larger than granulated. May contain calcium stearate also.	Same as for powder; disperses easily and evenly.
Onion Salt	Pure granulated onion with table salt.	Same as for powder. Also, a table condiment.
Minced	Particles approximately 1/8″; roughly equivalent to "finely minced."	Essentially same as for powder, but use when some texture of onion is desired. May be sautéed. Excellent in egg, tuna and potato salads, meat loaves, chili, breads, noodles, and vegetables.
Diced—1/4 inch	Particles approximately 1/4″ in size.	All-purpose when texture and appearance, as well as flavor, are desirable. Sautées well. Makes good raw relish for hamburgers. Use in sauces, soups, stuffed vegetables, stuffings, croquettes.
Diced—3/8 inch	Particles approximately 3/8″ in size.	All-purpose; excellent in barbecue beef, gravies, soups, casseroles, sautéed fish.
Chopped	Roughly Equivalent to "medium-chopped" in recipe terms.	Same as above; used when a chopped, rather than diced, texture and appearance is desirable. Sprinkle over green salads and hamburgers. Use in stews, pot roasts, marinades.
Large-chopped	Roughly equivalent to "coarse-chopped" in recipe terms.	Same as above, only more so.
Sliced	Mostly elongated, sliced pieces, some rings.	Same as above and especially for hash browns, liver and onions, French onion soup, and other dishes calling for very prominent onion appearance.
Large-sliced	Large-sliced, elongated pieces and rings.	Same as above only more so.
Toasted	All particle sizes are available in toasted form.	Whenever the additional flavor of browned onions will enhance a dish.

DEHYDRATED GARLIC
(including shallots)

Types	Descriptions	Seasoning Uses
GARLIC:		
Powder	Fine powder, often with calcium stearate added for free flow.	Whenever immediate garlic flavor is desired without noticeable particles. Use in dressings, sauces, garlic bread, salads. Rub into poultry, roasts, steaks, and chops. Use as final seasoning.
Granulated	Approximate consistency of granulated sugar; often with calcium stearate.	Same as for powder; flows especially well.
Ground	Slightly coarser than granulated; often with calcium stearate.	Same as for powder; free flowing, very dispersible.
Garlic Salt	Pure granulated garlic with table salt added.	Sprinkle over French fries, steak, fried chicken, chops, vegetables, bread.
Minced	Very finely minced, averaging about 1/16″ in size.	All-purpose flavoring; may be sautéed. Especially good in dressings, salads, relishes, casseroles, sauces, seafood, stuffings.
Chopped	Pieces roughly 1/4″ in size.	All-purpose; excellent for sautéeing. Use in long-cooking dishes, marinades.
Large-sliced	Solid slices, or "chips," roughly 1/2″ to 1″ in size.	Same as above. Insert into meats before roasting.
CHIVES:		
Freeze-dried	1/8″ pieces.	With sour cream for baked potatoes, cottage cheese, salads, spreads, sauces, eggs. Sprinkle over steaks, chops, salads.
SHALLOTS:		
Freeze-dried	3/8″ dice.	Vegetables, sauces, stocks, salad dressings, casseroles.

FLAVORING EXTRACTS

There is a large variety of flavoring extracts on the market today. Availability depends to some extent on which supplier you deal with. The following list is based on extracts generally included in foodservice and commercial baking price lists. A pure extract means a simple extraction of the essential flavor constituents of a natural product. In some cases, however, it is not chemically or practically feasible to achieve a natural extract, and, therefore, a reinforced or imitation flavor becomes the norm. In the following list, those which are more typically imitation flavor are indicated by "I;" all others are available as pure extracts (though there usually are imitation versions of them as well).

Flavors	Seasoning Uses
Almond	Fruit pies, cakes, macaroons, puddings.
Apricot (I)	Gelatins, fillings, frostings, cakes.
Banana (I)	Custards, creamy puddings, bread puddings, sweet breads, cakes, cream pies.
Black Walnut (I)	Cakes, fillings, icings, ice cream, rice puddings.
Blackberry	Fruit gelatins, ice cream sauces, sorbets, fruit cup.
Blueberry	Over strawberries, fruit pies, steamed puddings, stewed dried fruits.
Brandy (I)	Fruit cakes, mincemeat, dessert sauces, cream pies.
Butter Pecan (I)	Yellow cakes, chocolate pies, pecan pie fillings, butter fillings, cookies.
Cherry	Dessert sauces, cold beverages, applesauce, fruit salad dressings, pies.
Coconut (I)	Over sliced oranges, white cakes, cheesecakes, chocolate cakes, sweet breads, Danish pastries.
Coffee	Chocolate puddings, cakes, fillings, frostings, sauces.

Flavors	Seasoning Uses
Cointreau	Fresh fruit cups, cake fillings, crepes, sauces, frostings, fruit pies.
Lemon	Cakes, puddings, frostings, glazes, hot cross buns.
Lime	Fruit gelatin salads, fruit cups, pies, sorbets, fruit custards.
Maple (I)	Pies, cakes, puddings, candies, frostings.
Maple Walnut (I)	Cake fillings, frostings, tarts, Danish pastries, creams.
Orange	White cakes, pies, fillings, sauces for poultry and game as well as desserts, icings.
Peach	Frostings, fillings, sweet sauces, cream pies.
Peppermint	Chocolate puddings, frostings, sauces, jellies, cream pies.
Pineapple	Cakes, pies, dessert sauces, puddings, almond tarts, fruit cups and beverages.
Pistachio (I)	Cakes, fillings, icings, rich butter cookies, custard fillings.
Raspberry	Fruit cups, compotes, fillings, icings.
Rum (I)	Dessert sauces, rum balls, black bottom pies, cheesecakes, eggnog pies.

FLAVORING EXTRACTS (cont.d.)

Flavors	Seasoning Uses
Sherry (I)	Sauces, creamed soups, seafood and poultry casseroles, puddings.
Strawberry	Meringues, tortes, brownies, stewed pears, baked peaches, cakes, pies.
Tangerine	Fruit sauces, melon cups, ambrosia, baked apples, pies.
Vanilla	Cakes, puddings, whenever chocolate is used, fruit compotes and desserts, pancakes, cookies, muffins, pies, dessert sauces, frostings.

APPETIZERS

Liptauer Cheese

Yield: 14 cups

Featured Seasonings: powdered mustard, sour cream, onion powder, caraway seeds, capers, anchovies, paprika, salt, ground red pepper

Ingredients	Quantities	Procedure
Powdered mustard	1/4 cup	1. Combine powdered mustard with warm water; let stand 10 minutes for flavor to develop.
Warm water	1/4 cup	
Butter or margarine, softened	2 pounds	2. In a mixing bowl cream butter with cheeses.
Cream cheese, softened	2 pounds	
Creamed cottage cheese	1 quart	
Dairy sour cream	2 cups	3. Add mustard along with remaining ingredients and blend well.
Onion powder	1/2 cup	4. Chill and serve. Or spoon into molds. Refrigerate until firm. Unmold and garnish with parsley flakes. Serve with crackers, if desired.
Caraway seeds	1/3 cup	
Capers, chopped	1/3 cup	
Anchovies, minced	16	
Paprika	1/4 cup	
Salt	1/2 teaspoon	
Ground red pepper	1/4 teaspoon	

Anchoyade (French Anchovy Tarts)

Yield: 12 dozen

Featured Seasonings: onion, parsley flakes, garlic powder, tomato paste, lemon juice, ground black pepper

Ingredients	Quantities	Procedure
Instant minced onion	1/4 cup	1. Rehydrate minced onion in water for 10 minutes.
Water	1/4 cup	
Anchovy fillets	8 (2 oz.) cans	2. Drain anchovies. Place anchovies in a bowl; mash.
Cream cheese, softened	12 ounces	3. Add onion to anchovies along with cream cheese, parsley flakes, garlic powder, oil, tomato paste, lemon juice, and black pepper; mix thoroughly. Stir in bread crumbs; set aside.
Parsley flakes	1/4 cup	
Garlic powder	2 tablespoons	
Olive oil	1/2 cup	
Tomato paste	2 tablespoons	
Lemon juice	4 teaspoons	
Ground black pepper	1/2 teaspoon	
Soft bread crumbs	1 quart	
Prepared pastry dough	4 pounds	4. On a lightly floured board, roll out pastry 1/8-inch thick. Cut into circles 1/4-inch wider all around than tops of thumbsize metal shells. Fit pastry into shells without stretching pastry. Trim top edges flush with shells.

5. Fill with anchovy mixture, piling mixture high. Place shells on baking sheet.
6. Bake in a preheated 400°F. oven until golden, about 12 minutes.
7. Remove the canapes from the metal shells and serve hot, sprinkled with parsley flakes if desired.

Spiced Chick Peas

Yield: 48 portions

Featured Seasonings: onion, ground black pepper, salt, garlic

Ingredients	Quantities	Procedure
Instant minced onion	1/3 cup	1. Rehydrate onion in water for 10 minutes.
Water	1/3 cup	
Canned chick peas, drained	6 (20 oz.) cans	2. Combine onion with remaining ingredients; toss gently.
Ground black pepper	1 1/2 teaspoons	3. Serve as an hors d'oeuvre, salad, etc.
Salt	3/4 teaspoon	
Instant garlic powder	1/2 teaspoon	

Caraway Cheese Sticks

Yield:	9 dozen
Featured Seasonings:	onion powder, garlic powder, ground red pepper, caraway seeds

Ingredients	Quantities	Procedure
All-purpose flour	3 cups	1. In a mixing bowl, combine flour with onion and garlic powders, and red pepper.
Onion powder	3 tablespoons	
Garlic powder	3/4 teaspoon	
Ground red pepper	3/4 teaspoon	
Sharp cheddar cheese, shredded	3 cups	2. Add cheese, butter, and caraway seeds. Mix with pastry blender or fork; shape into a ball. Cover and refrigerate at least 15 minutes.
Butter or margarine, softened	1 1/2 cups	
Caraway seeds	1 tablespoon	
		3. On a lightly floured board, roll dough 1/4-inch thick. Cut into strips 4-inches long by 3/4-inch wide. Roll or twist slightly. Place on ungreased baking sheets.
		4. Bake in a preheated 375°F. oven until golden, about 10 minutes.

Captain's Fish Appetizer

Yield: 48 portions

Featured Seasonings: lemon juice, tarragon vinegar, bay leaves, salt, black peppercorns, sour cream, curry powder, garlic salt, capers, red bell peppers or pimientos

Ingredients	Quantities	Procedure
Frozen cod fillets	8 pounds	1. Place frozen block cod fillets in skillet with water, vinegar, bay leaves, salt, and peppercorns. Bring to the boiling point. Reduce heat and simmer, covered, until fish becomes opaque and flakes easily with fork.
Water	2 quarts	
Lemon juice	8 lemons, divided	
Tarragon vinegar	1/2 cup	
Bay leaves	8	
Salt	2 tablespoons	2. Remove fish from liquid with slotted spatula. Chill and cut into cubes.
Black peppercorns	1 tablespoon	
Mayonnaise	1 quart	3. Combine mayonnaise, sour cream, curry, garlic salt, apple, and capers; chill.
Sour cream, dairy	1 quart	
Curry powder	2 tablespoons	4. To serve, place in each appetizer dish 1 or 2 lettuce leaves and 1 tablespoon chopped egg.
Garlic salt	1 tablespoon	
Apples, chopped	4	5. Add a layer of fish. Top with 1 tablespoon dressing. Repeat layers once more.
Dill pickle, chopped	1/2 cup	
Capers	2 tablespoons	6. Garnish with chopped egg and red pepper or pimiento.
Hard-cooked eggs, chopped	12	
Lettuce leaves	As needed	
Red Bell peppers, chopped or	4 red peppers or	
Pimiento, chopped	1 cup pimiento	

Piroshki (Herbed, Meat-Filled Crescents)

Yield: 12 dozen

Featured Seasonings: onion, dill weed, parsley flakes, salt, paprika, ground black pepper, lemon juice

Ingredients	Quantities	Procedure
Butter or margarine	1/3 cup	1. Melt butter in a skillet. Add onion; sauté for 2 minutes. Add beef; cook and stir until brown, about 4 minutes.
Onions, minced	2/3 cup	
Ground beef	1 pound	
Hard-cooked eggs, chopped	4	2. Remove skillet from heat; stir in eggs, dill weed, parsley, salt, paprika, and black pepper. Add sour cream and lemon juice; mix thoroughly; set aside.
Dill weed	2 tablespoons	
Parsley flakes	2 tablespoons	
Salt	1 1/2 teaspoons	
Paprika	1 teaspoon	
Ground black pepper	1/4 teaspoon	
Dairy sour cream	1/4 cup	
Lemon juice	2 teaspoons	
Frozen patty shells, thawed	1 (2 lb. 8 oz.) package	3. On a lightly floured board, press together half of the patty shells; roll out 1/8-inch thick. Cut into 2-inch rounds.
		4. Place a scant teaspoon of meat mixture on each round; moisten edges lightly with water. Pinch together, forming a half moon. Repeat, using remaining packages of patty shells and remaining meat mixture. Place on ungreased baking pans.
		5. Bake in a preheated 400°F. oven until golden, about 12 minutes. Serve hot.
		6. Unbaked Piroshkis may be freezer-wrapped and frozen for up to 2 months. Defrost and bake as above.

Empanadas

Yield: 50 turnovers

Featured Seasonings: onion, chili powder, salt, paprika, oregano leaves

Ingredients	Quantities	Procedure
Instant minced onion	1 1/4 cups	1. Rehydrate minced onion in water for 10 minutes; set aside.
Water	1 1/4 cups	
Olive or salad oil	2/3 cup	2. In a large skillet, heat oil until hot. Add onion and beef; sauté for 5 minutes. Drain off excess fat.
Ground beef	5 pounds	
Canned tomatoes, broken up	1/2 (No. 10) can	3. Stir in tomatoes, raisins, olives, chili powder, salt, paprika, and oregano. Cook uncovered for 5 minutes, stirring constantly. Remove from heat; stir in eggs; cool.
Raisins or currants	1 1/4 cups	
Pitted green olives, chopped	1 1/4 cups	
Chili powder	2/3 cup	
Salt	3 tablespoons	
Paprika	3 tablespoons	
Oregano leaves, crumbled	1 1/2 tablespoons	
Hard-cooked eggs, chopped	15	
Pastry dough, prepared	7 1/2 pounds	4. Divide pastry into 50 parts. On a lightly floured board, roll each portion separately into a 6-inch circle, 1/8 inch thick.

5. Spoon about 1/3-cup meat mixture onto one side of each circle; moisten edges with water; fold pastry over filling to form a semicircle; press edges to seal and crimp.

6. Prick tops of pastries to allow steam to escape. (If desired, brush tops with egg yolk beaten with water.) Place on baking sheets.

7. Bake in preheated 400°F. oven until golden, about 30 minutes. Serve hot.

Calzone (Meat and Cheese Turnovers)

Yield: 120

Featured Seasonings: onion powder, garlic powder, ground oregano, ground black pepper, olive oil

Ingredients	Quantities	Procedure
Prepared pizza dough	6 pounds	1. Roll pizza dough 1/8-inch thick on a lightly floured board; cut into 4-inch circles.
Italian salami, thinly sliced	1 1/2 pounds	
Mozzarella cheese	3 pounds	2. Cut salami into 1 1/2-inch strips and cheese into 1-inch strips.
Onion powder	As needed	3. Place a few pieces of salami and cheese on one side of each round.
Garlic powder	As needed	4. Sprinkle with onion powder, garlic powder, oregano, a dash of black pepper, and a few drops of oil.
Ground oregano	As needed	
Ground black pepper	As needed	5. Fold dough over the filling; press edges firmly together. Repeat.
Olive oil	As needed	
Milk	As needed	

6. Place on a greased baking sheet; brush tops with milk and bake in a preheated 350 °F. oven 25 to 30 minutes or until nicely browned.

Scotch Eggs

Yield: 48 eggs

Featured Seasoning: Worcestershire sauce

Ingredients	Quantities	Procedure
Hard-cooked eggs	48	1. Peel eggs; dust with flour.
Flour	1 cup	
Bulk sausage meat	8 pounds	2. Mix sausage meat with Worcestershire sauce; divide into 48 equal parts. Shape each part into a flat cake; mold evenly around one egg, making sure there are no cracks in sausage meat.
Worcestershire sauce	3/4 cup	
Uncooked eggs, lightly beaten	8	3. Dip into beaten egg; roll in bread crumbs, gently patting bread crumbs in place. Repeat.
Fine dry bread crumbs	1 1/2 quarts	
Deep fat for frying	As needed	4. Preheat fat to 325 °F. Add a few eggs at a time and fry until sausage is cooked and golden, about 7 minutes.
		5. Drain on paper towels. Serve hot or cold.

Eggplant Caviar

Yield: 2 1/2 quarts

Featured Seasonings: olive oil, vinegar, onion powder, tomato paste, salt, garlic powder, ground black pepper, sesame seed

Ingredients	Quantities	Procedure
Eggplants	6 pounds	1. Peel eggplants. Place in baking pan; cover with foil. Bake in a preheated 400°F. oven until tender, about 1 hour. Remove from oven; cool slightly. 2. Cut eggplants into chunks.
Olive oil	1 1/8 cup	3. Mash eggplants until smooth. Add remaining ingredients except sesame seeds; blend well.
Vinegar	3/4 cup	
Onion powder	3/4 cup	
Tomato paste	1/3 cup	
Salt	2 tablespoons	
Sugar	2 tablespoons	
Garlic powder	1 tablespoon	
Ground black pepper	1 1/2 teaspoons	
Sesame seeds, toasted	3/4 cup	4. Turn into serving bowl. Stir in sesame seeds; Chill. 5. Serve as a dip or spread with crackers or vegetable sticks, if desired.

SOUPS

Sopa Mejicana de Pollo (Mexican Chicken Soup)

Yield:	3 gallons
Featured Seasonings:	onion, garlic, carrots, salt, chili powder, ground cumin, ground red pepper

Ingredients	Quantities	Procedure
Canned condensed chicken broth	2 1/2 (50 oz.) cans	1. In a sauce pot, combine chicken broth, water, chicken broth mix, tomatoes, and minced onion and garlic; bring to the boiling point.
Water	2 1/2 cans	
Chicken flavor broth mix	1/4 cup	
Canned tomatoes, broken up	1/2 (No. 10) can	
Instant minced onion	3/4 cup	
Instant minced garlic	1 1/2 teaspoons	
Chicken breasts, skinned, boned, and cut into 1/2-inch chunks	4 pounds	2. Stir in chicken, carrots, salt, chili powder, cumin, and red pepper. Return to the boiling point. Reduce heat and simmer, covered, until chicken and carrots are tender, about 15 minutes.
Carrots, thinly sliced	2 1/2 quarts	
Salt	1 1/2 tablespoons	
Chili powder	1 tablespoon	
Ground cumin seed	1 tablespoon	
Ground red pepper	1 teaspoon	3. Stir in peas and zucchini. Cover and simmer for 3 minutes.
Green peas	1 1/2 quarts	4. Serve garnished with avocado chunks, if desired.
Zucchini, sliced	1 1/2 quarts	

Gingered Chicken Soup

Yield: 48 portions

Featured Seasonings: ground ginger, onion flakes

Ingredients	Quantities	Procedure
Rich chicken broth	2 gallons	1. In a sauce pot combine chicken broth, chicken, and ginger; simmer for 15 minutes.
Chicken, cooked and slivered	2 quarts	
Ground ginger	3 tablespoons	
Onion flakes	1 1/2 quarts	2. Rehydrate onion in water for 10 minutes.
Water	5 1/3 cups	
Oil, salad	1 cup	3. In a medium skillet heat oil until hot. Add onions and bean sprouts; sauté for 5 minutes, stirring.
Bean sprouts, drained	1 gallon	
		4. Add sautéed vegetables to broth; simmer, covered, for 15 minutes.
Hard-cooked eggs, sliced	16	5. Ladle soup into bowls; garnish each serving with 2 or 3 slices of egg.

Canadian Habitant Pea Soup

Yield:	3 gallons
Featured Seasonings:	carrots, onion flakes, mixed vegetable flakes, salt, ground allspice, ground black pepper, parsley flakes

Ingredients	Quantities	Procedure
Dried yellow split peas	6 pounds	1. Rinse split peas; drain well.
Water	3 3/4 gallons	2. In a sauce pot combine peas and water; bring to the boiling point; skim off foam.
Carrots, diced	3 quarts	3. Add carrots, salt pork, onion flakes, mixed vegetable flakes, salt, allspice, and black pepper. Simmer, covered, for 3 hours.
Salt pork, diced	3 pounds	
Onion flakes	3 cups	
Mixed vegetable flakes	3 cups	
Salt	1/3 cup	
Ground allspice	1 tablespoon	
Ground black pepper	1 1/2 teaspoons	
Parsley flakes	1 1/4 cups	4. Add parsley flakes and serve.

Caribbean Pea Soup

Yield:	3 gallons
Featured Seasonings:	carrots, onion flakes, salt, parsley flakes, thyme leaves, ground nutmeg, ground black pepper

Ingredients	Quantities	Procedure
Split peas	2 1/2 cups	1. Rinse split peas; drain well; set aside.
Oil, salad	1 cup	2. In a sauce pot, heat oil until hot; add chuck; sauté until brown.
Boneless chuck, cut into 1/2-inch pieces	7 1/2 pounds	
Water	2 1/2 gallons	3. Add water, carrots, onion flakes, salt, parsley, thyme, nutmeg, black pepper, and the reserved split peas. Bring to a boil. Reduce heat and simmer, covered, for 50 minutes.
Large carrots, sliced	5	
Onion flakes	1 1/2 cups	
Salt	1/3 cup	
Parsley flakes	1/3 cup	
Thyme leaves	2 tablespoons	
Ground nutmeg	1 1/4 teaspoons	
Ground black pepper	1 1/4 teaspoons	
White potatoes, cubed and peeled	3 cups	4. Add white and sweet potatoes. Simmer, covered, for 10 minutes.
Sweet potatoes, cubed and peeled	3 cups	
Fresh spinach, chopped	1 pound	5. Add spinach; simmer until vegetables are tender, about 3 minutes.

African Peanut Soup

Yield: about 3 gallons

Featured Seasonings: onion powder, bay leaves, ground red pepper

Ingredients	Quantities	Procedure
Butter or margarine	1 1/4 cups	1. In a sauce pot melt butter. Stir in flour; cook until lightly browned. Remove from heat.
Flour	2 cups	
Chicken broth	3 gallons	2. Stir in chicken broth, onion powder, bay leaves, and red pepper. Bring to the boiling point. Reduce heat and simmer, uncovered, for 10 minutes.
Onion powder	3 tablespoons	
Bay leaves	10 small	
Ground red pepper	1 teaspoon	
Crunchy peanut butter	2 quarts	3. Stir in peanut butter. Simmer 5 minutes longer. Remove bay leaves.
		4. Serve sprinkled with chopped peanuts, if desired.

Greek Minted Yogurt Soup

Yield: about 3 gallons

Featured Seasonings: mint flakes, salt

Ingredients	Quantities	Procedure
Raw regular cooking rice	1 quart	1. In a sauce pot combine rice, flour, mint flakes, and salt. Stir in eggs. Add broth; mix well.
Flour	1/2 cup	
Mint flakes, crumbled	1/3 cup	2. Bring to the boiling point, stirring constantly. Simmer, covered, until rice is tender, about 20 minutes, stirring occasionally.
Salt	2 tablespoons	
Eggs, lightly beaten	8	
Chicken broth	2 gallons	3. Stir in yogurt. Heat, but do not boil, stirring constantly.
Plain yogurt	2 quarts	4. Soup may be served hot or cold, topped with a dollop of yogurt, if desired.

Ciorba Cu Perisoare (Rumanian Vegetable Soup with Pork Dumplings)

Yield: 48 to 60 portions

Featured Seasonings: parsley flakes, dill seeds, paprika, ground black pepper, salt, garlic powder

Ingredients	Quantities	Procedure
Chicken broth	3 gallons	1. In a sauce pot bring broth to the boiling point. Add vegetables, 3/4-cup of the parsley flakes, dill seeds, paprika, and black pepper. Simmer, covered, for 30 minutes.
Sauerkraut, rinsed and drained	1/2 (No. 10) can	
Canned tomatoes, broken up	1/2 (No. 10) can	
Green beans, cut into 1-inch pieces	2 pounds	
Cauliflowerettes	3 quarts	
Carrots, sliced	3 quarts	
Parsley flakes, divided	1 1/4 cups	
Dill seeds	1/3 cup	
Paprika	2 tablespoons	
Ground black pepper	1 1/2 teaspoons	
Ground lean pork	9 pounds	2. Meanwhile, in a mixing bowl combine pork, rice, eggs, salt, garlic powder, and remaining 1/2-cup parsley flakes; mix lightly. Shape into 1 1/2-inch balls. Drop meatballs into boiling water; cook for 5 minutes. Add meatballs to soup; simmer 15 minutes longer.
Rice, cooked	2 1/4 quarts	
Eggs, beaten	12	
Salt	2 tablespoons	
Garlic powder	1 1/2 teaspoons	
Boiling water	1 1/2 gallons	3. Serve with sour cream, if desired.

Swedish Fruit Soup

Yield: 48 portions

Featured Seasonings: lemon juice, ground or stick cinnamon, salt

Ingredients	Quantities	Procedure
Oranges, peeled, sliced, and quartered	6 medium	1. In a sauce pot combine oranges, lemons, raisins, lemon juice, cinnamon, and 3 quarts of the water. Bring to the boiling point. Reduce heat and simmer, uncovered, for 20 minutes. Remove cinnamon sticks.
Lemons, thinly sliced and quartered	8	
Seedless raisins	3 cups	
Lemon juice	1 1/2 cups	
Cinnamon sticks, (2-inch) or ground cinnamon	6 sticks or 2 tablespoons ground	
Water, divided	3 1/4 quarts	
Canned sliced peaches	1/2 (No. 10) can	2. Drain peaches, reserving liquid. Cut each slice in half. Add peaches, peach liquid, undrained cherries, sugar, and salt to sauce pot. Return mixture to a boil.
Canned pitted tart cherries	6 (20 oz.) cans	
Sugar	2/3 cup	
Salt	1/2 teaspoon	
Cornstarch	1/3 cup	3. Mix cornstarch with remaining 1 cup water. Stir into the fruit mixture. Cook and stir until clear, about 1 minute.
		4. Chill.
		5. Serve garnished with whipped cream, if desired.

Mulligatawny Soup

Yield: 48 portions

Featured Seasonings: celery, onions, carrots, curry powder, garlic powder, salt, ground cumin seed, ground cardamom, ground ginger, lemon juice

Ingredients	Quantities	Procedure
Butter or margarine	1 1/4 cups	1. Heat butter in a large sauce pot. Add celery, onions, and carrots; sauté for 5 minutes. Add curry powder, garlic powder, and water. Cover and cook for 10 minutes.
Celery, chopped	1 1/2 quarts	
Onions, chopped	1 1/2 quarts	
Carrots, thinly sliced	2 cups	
Curry Powder	1/3 cup	
Garlic Powder	1 1/2 teaspoons	
Water	1 1/2 quarts	
Canned condensed chicken broth	4 (50 oz.) cans	2. Add chicken broth and split peas. Cover and simmer for 1 hour.
Yellow split peas	4 1/2 cups	
Salt	1 tablespoon	3. Stir in salt and remaining spices 10 minutes before cooking time is up.
Ground cumin seeds	1 tablespoon	
Ground cardamom	1 1/2 teaspoons	4. Remove from heat. Push through a coarse sieve, if desired.
Ground ginger	1 1/2 teaspoons	
Milk	3 quarts	5. Stir in milk, cream, and lemon juice. Heat only until hot. DO NOT BOIL.
Heavy cream	2 cups	
Lemon juice	2 tablespoons	

Kal Bi Gui (Korean Short Ribs Soup)

Yield: about 4 1/2 gallons

Featured Seasonings: onion powder, garlic powder, ground ginger, salt, ground red pepper, carrots, scallions

Ingredients	Quantities	Procedure
Water	4 gallons	1. In a large sauce pot combine water and short ribs. Bring to the boiling point; skim off foam. Cover and simmer until meat is tender, 1 1/2 to 2 hours.
Short ribs of beef, cut into 1-inch pieces	24 pounds	
Onion powder	1 1/2 cups	2. Stir in onion and garlic powders, ginger, salt, and red pepper. Add spinach, carrots, and scallions; simmer for 10 minutes.
Garlic powder	3 tablespoons	
Ground ginger	2 tablespoons	
Salt	1 tablespoon	
Ground red pepper	1 1/2 teaspoons	
Fresh spinach, torn	6 pounds	
Carrots, thinly sliced	12	
Scallions (green onions), cut into 2-inch pieces	3 quarts	
Eggs, beaten	12	3. Bring to a boil; slowly stir in eggs.
		4. Remove from heat and serve.

Soupe de Poisson (French Seafood Soup)

Yield:	about 3 gallons
Featured Seasonings:	onion, garlic, tomato puree, dry white wine, salt, mint leaves, basil leaves, saffron, ground black pepper, parsley flakes

Ingredients	Quantities	Procedure
Instant minced onion	1 cup	1. Rehydrate minced onion and garlic in water for 10 minutes.
Instant minced garlic	1/4 cup	
Water	1 cup	
Oil, olive	2 cups	2. In a large sauce pot, heat oil until hot. Add onion and garlic; saute until golden, 5 minutes.
Canned tomatoes, broken up	2 (No. 10) cans	3. Stir in tomatoes, tomato purée, clam broth, wine, salt, mint, basil, sugar, saffron, and black pepper.
Tomato puree	1 (No. 10) can	
Clam broth	16 (8 oz.) bottles	4. Bring to the boiling point. Reduce heat and simmer, uncovered, for 10 minutes.
Dry white wine	2 quarts	
Salt	1/4 cup	
Mint leaves, crumbled	2 1/2 tablespoons	
Basil leaves, crumbled	2 1/2 tablespoons	
Sugar	2 1/2 tablespoons	
Saffron, crumbled	4 teaspoons	
Ground black pepper	1 teaspoon	
Cod fillets, cut into chunks	8 pounds	5. Stir in cod, shrimp, and scallops. Return to the boiling point. Reduce heat and simmer, covered, for 5 minutes. Add lobster and clams. Return to the boiling point. Reduce heat and simmer, covered, until clams open and lobster turns red, about 5 minutes.
Raw shrimp, peeled and deveined	4 pounds	
Scallops	4 pounds	
Rock lobster tails, removed from shells and cut into large pieces	9 pounds	
Little neck clams, scrubbed	8 dozen	
Parsley flakes	2 cups	6. Sprinkle with parsley. Serve with French bread.

MEATS

Cocido Serrano (Beef and Vegetable Stew from Colombia)

Yield: 48 portions

Featured Seasonings: cider vinegar, onion, salt, cumin seeds, bay leaves, ground red pepper, whole black peppercorns, oregano leaves, saffron

Ingredients	Quantities	Procedure
Stew beef, cut into 1/2 inch pieces	16 pounds	1. Dredge beef with flour.
Flour	2 cups	
Oil, salad	1/2 cup	2. In a large sauce pot heat oil until hot. Add meat, brown well.
Water	1 1/2 gallons	3. Add water, vinegar, minced onion, salt, cumin, bay leaves, red and black peppers. Simmer, covered, until meat is almost tender, about 1 1/2 hours.
Cider vinegar	1/3 cup	
Instant minced onion	2 cups	
Salt	1/3 cup	4. Remove meat; keep warm.
Cumin seeds	2 tablespoons	
Bay leaves	8	
Ground red pepper	2 teaspoons	
Whole black peppercorns	2 teaspoons	
Tomatoes, sliced into wedges	5 pounds	5. To stew liquid, add tomatoes, potatoes, carrots, green beans, corn, oregano, and saffron.
Medium potatoes, peeled and quartered	4 pounds	
Large carrots, cut into 1-inch pieces	2 pounds	6. Return meat to pot. Cover and cook until meat and vegetables are tender, about 30 minutes longer.
Green beans, cut into 1-inch pieces	2 pounds	
Ears of corn, cut into 2-inch pieces	32	7. Serve stew with corn holders or toothpicks, if desired.
Oregano leaves	4 teaspoons	
Saffron, crumbled	2 teaspoons	

Carbonnade Flamande (Belgian Beef Stew Cooked in Beer)

Yield: 48 portions

Featured Seasonings: onions, beer, salt, garlic, ground nutmeg, ground thyme, ground black pepper

Ingredients	Quantities	Procedure
Lean stew beef, cut into 2-inch cubes	20 pounds	1. Dredge beef cubes in flour; set aside.
Flour	2 2/3 cups	
Butter or margarine, divided	1 pound	2. In a heavy sauce pot, melt half the butter.
Onions, chopped	1 quart	3. Add onions and garlic; sauté until lightly browned. Remove and set aside.
Garlic, minced	2 teaspoons	
		4. Add remaining butter to sauce pot. Add beef cubes; brown well on all sides.
Beer	8 (12 oz.) cans	5. Return onions to sauce pot. Add remaining ingredients. Simmer, covered, until meat is tender, about 1 1/2 hours.
Salt	1/3 cup	
Ground nutmeg	2 teaspoons	
Ground thyme	2 teaspoons	
Ground black pepper	2 teaspoons	

Stifado

Yield: 48 portions

Featured Seasonings: onions, tomato paste, cider vinegar, ground or stick cinnamon, whole cloves, salt, ground black pepper

Ingredients	Quantities	Procedure
Olive or salad oil	1 1/2 cups	1. In a heavy sauce pot, heat oil until hot. Add meat; brown well on all sides.
Beef stew meat, cut into 2-inch pieces	20 pounds	
Onions, chopped	2 quarts	2. Add onions to meat; sauté for 3 minutes.
Water	1 gallon	3. Stir in remaining ingredients. Bring to the boiling point. Reduce heat and simmer, covered, until meat is tender, 1 1/2 to 2 hours.
Tomato paste	8 (6 oz.) cans	
Cider vinegar	1 1/2 cups	
Cinnamon sticks, (4-inch) broken in half	8 sticks	
or	or	
Ground cinnamon	2 tablespoons	
Whole cloves	36	
Salt	1/3 cup	
Ground black pepper	4 teaspoons	

Steakhouse Stew

Yield: 48 portions

Featured Seasonings: onions, tomato sauce, Worcestershire sauce, vinegar, tomato paste, salt

Ingredients	Quantities	Procedure
Lean stew beef, cut into 1-inch cubes	16 pounds	1. Dredge beef cubes with flour; set aside.
Flour	2 cups	
Oil, salad	1 1/2 cups	2. In a large, heavy sauce pot, heat oil until hot. Add beef cubes and onions; brown well on all sides, turning often.
Onions, coarsely chopped	2 quarts	
Tomato sauce	2 quarts	3. Stir in remaining ingredients, except mushrooms. Bring to the boiling point, stirring occasionally.
Water	1 1/2 quarts	
Worcestershire sauce	1 1/2 cups	4. Reduce heat and simmer, covered, until meat is tender, 1 1/2 to 2 hours, stirring occasionally.
Vinegar	1 cup	
Tomato paste	1 cup	
Sugar	1 cup	
Salt	1 tablespoon	
Mushrooms, sliced	2 (1 lb.) cans	5. Add mushrooms; heat only until hot.
		6. Serve over cooked noodles, if desired.

71

Spanish Beef Stew

Yield: 48 portions

Featured Seasonings: olive oil, onion flakes, garlic, dry white wine, salt, paprika, bay leaves, thyme leaves, ground cinnamon, ground black pepper

Ingredients	Quantities	Procedure
Boneless stew beef	20 pounds	1. Cut meat into 2-inch cubes.
Olive oil, divided	2 cups	2. In a heavy sauce pot, heat 1 cup of the oil. Add half of the meat at a time; brown well over high heat. Remove meat from pot; set aside.
Onion flakes	2 2/3 cups	3. Meanwhile, rehydrate onion flakes and minced garlic in 2 cups water; let stand for 10 minutes.
Instant minced garlic	2 tablespoons	
Water	As directed	
Large tomatoes, diced	8	4. Heat remaining 1 cup oil in sauce pot. Add rehydrated onion and garlic; sauté for 5 minutes. Add tomatoes and wine. Cook over high heat until liquid evaporates, stirring constantly. Reduce heat.
Dry white wine	1 quart	
Flour	1 cup	5. Add flour; cook and stir until brown.
Salt	1/4 cup	6. Blend in remaining seasonings, meat, and 2 quarts boiling water. Cover and simmer, stirring occasionally, until meat is tender, about 2 hours. (Add more water, if necessary, during cooking period.)
Paprika	1 tablespoon	
Small bay leaves	8	
Thyme leaves, crumbled	2 tablespoons	
Ground cinnamon	2 teaspoons	7. Before serving, remove meat to serving platter; strain sauce over it.
Ground black pepper	1 teaspoon	
		8. Serve with boiled potatoes and garnish with pine nuts, if desired.

Kaeng Kari Nua (Curried Beef Stew)

Yield: 48 portions

Featured Seasonings: flaked coconut, bay leaves, onion powder, ground turmeric, paprika, salt, garlic, lemon peel, ground red pepper, ground caraway seeds, ground coriander, ground anise, ground cinnamon

Ingredients	Quantities	Procedure
Flaked coconut	8 (8 oz.) cans	1. Combine coconut and water; let stand for one hour.
Boiling water	1 gallon	2. Drain, reserving liquid and coconut separately; set aside.
Oil, salad	1 cup	3. In a heavy sauce pot, heat oil until hot. Add meat; brown well.
Lean boneless beef shoulder, cut into 1-inch cubes	12 pounds	
Bay leaves	16	4. Combine remaining ingredients; stir into meat.
Flour	1 cup	5. Gradually add reserved coconut liquid.
Onion powder	1/3 cup	6. Bring to the boil, stirring constantly.
Ground turmeric	1/4 cup	7. Reduce heat and simmer, covered, until meat is tender, about
Paprika	1/4 cup	1 1/2 hours.
Salt	2 tablespoons	8. Taste, adding additional red pepper if desired.
Garlic, minced	2 tablespoons	9. Serve with hot boiled rice garnished with reserved shredded
Lemon peel, grated	2 tablespoons	coconut.
Ground red pepper	2 to 4 teaspoons	
Ground caraway seeds	2 teaspoons	
Ground coriander	2 teaspoons	
Ground anise	2 teaspoons	
Ground cinnamon	2 teaspoons	
Boiled rice		

Agnisko Kapama (Lamb Vegetable Stew)

Yield: 48 portions

Featured Seasonings: onions, garlic, tomato paste, salt, paprika, ground black pepper, parsley, dill weed

Ingredients	Quantities	Procedure
Oil, salad	1 cup	1. In a large sauce pot, heat oil until hot.
Boneless lamb shoulder, cut into 1-inch		2. Add meat; brown well on all sides.
pieces	16 pounds	
Onions, minced	1 quart	3. Add onion and garlic; sauté until tender. Stir in flour.
Garlic, minced	4 teaspoons	
Flour	1 cup	
Water	1 gallon	4. Add water, tomato paste, salt, paprika, and black pepper. Bring to a boil.
Tomato paste	1/2 cup	
Salt	1/3 cup	
Paprika	1/4 cup	
Ground black pepper	2 teaspoons	
Potatoes, peeled and quartered	12 pounds	5. Reduce heat and simmer, covered, until meat is almost tender, about 1 1/2 hours. Add potatoes and carrots; simmer, covered, 1 hour longer.
Carrots, peeled and cut into 2-inch		
pieces	8 pounds	
Fresh mushrooms, sliced	4 pounds	6. Add mushrooms, parsley, and dill. Cook until meat and vegetables are tender, about 20 to 30 minutes longer. Serve with a dollop of yogurt, if desired.
Parsley, chopped	1 cup	
Dill weed, chopped	2 tablespoons	

English Beef Pie

Yield: 48 portions

Featured Seasonings: onions, Worcestershire sauce, salt, parsley

Ingredients	Quantities	Procedure
Stew beef, boneless, cut into 1-inch pieces	18 pounds	1. In a large sauce pot, brown beef in oil.
Oil	1 1/2 cups	
Onions, chopped	3 quarts	2. Add onions; sauté until tender.
Water, divided	3 quarts	3. Stir in 2 1/4 quarts of the water, Worcestershire sauce, and salt. Cook, uncovered, for 10 minutes, stirring frequently. Simmer, covered, for 30 minutes.
Worcestershire sauce	1 1/2 cups	
Salt	3 1/2 tablespoons	
Potatoes, peeled and diced	1 1/2 quarts	4. Add potatoes and carrots. Cook, covered, until meat and vegetables are tender, about 30 minutes.
Carrots, diced	1 1/2 quarts	
Flour	1 1/4 cups	5. Mix flour with remaining 3 cups water; gradually stir into meat mixture.
Mushrooms, sliced	3 pounds	6. Add mushrooms and parsley and cook until gravy is thickened. Turn into individual ovenproof casseroles.
Parsley, chopped	3/4 cup	
Prepared pie crust	4 pounds	7. Roll pastry 1/8-inch thick. Cut to fit tops of casseroles. Trim and flute edges. Make cuts in pastry for steam to escape.
Egg yolks	4	8. Combine egg yolk with water; brush over pastry. Bake in a preheated 425°F. oven for 20 minutes.
Water	3 tablespoons	
		9. Reduce temperature to 350°F. and bake until pastry is nicely browned, about 20 minutes.

Szekely Gulyas (Hungarian Pork Stew)

Yield: 48 to 64 portions

Featured Seasonings: onions, dry white wine, paprika, caraway seeds, salt, tarragon leaves, ground black pepper, sour cream, parsley

Ingredients	Quantities	Procedure
Bacon fat	1 1/2 cups	1. In a heavy, large sauce pot, heat bacon fat until hot. Add pork; brown on all sides, a few pieces at a time; remove and set aside.
Boneless pork shoulder, cut into 1-inch cubes	16 pounds	
Sauerkraut, rinsed and well-drained	16 pounds	2. To drippings left in sauce pot, add sauerkraut and onions; sauté until golden.
Onions, minced	1 quart	
Chicken broth	2 quarts	3. Return pork to sauce pot along with chicken broth, wine, paprika, caraway, salt, tarragon, and black pepper. Bring to the boiling point. Reduce heat and simmer, covered, until pork is tender, about 1 1/2 hours.
Dry white wine	1 1/2 quarts	
Paprika	1/2 cup	
Caraway seeds	2 tablespoons	
Salt	2 tablespoons	
Tarragon leaves, crumbled	1 tablespoon	
Ground black pepper	2 teaspoons	
Sour cream, dairy	2 quarts	4. Stir in sour cream. Heat until hot. *Do not boil.* Sprinkle with parsley.
Parsley, chopped	1 cup	5. Serve with cooked noodles, if desired.

Polish Mushroom and Meat Stew

Yield: 48 portions

Featured Seasonings: onion flakes, bay leaves, ground black pepper, sherry, Madeira, or dry red wine

Ingredients	Quantities	Procedure
Salt pork, diced	1 1/2 pounds	1. In a large, heavy sauce pot, cook salt pork until brown. Remove pork cracklings; set aside. Add sausage to fat in sauce pot and brown. Remove and set aside.
Polish sausage, cut into 1-inch slices	3 pounds	
Fresh mushrooms, sliced	6 pounds	2. Leave 1 1/2 cups fat in sauce pot; reserve 3/4 cup for later use. Add mushrooms to sauce pot; sauté for 5 minutes; remove and set aside.
Canned sauerkraut	1 1/2 (No. 10) cans	3. Drain sauerkraut, reserving liquid. Add sufficient water to sauerkraut liquid to measure 1 1/2 quarts; set aside. Add sauerkraut to sauce pot; sauté for 5 minutes; remove and set aside.
Flour	3/4 cup	4. To sauce pot add reserved 3/4 cup fat. Stir in flour and brown. Gradually stir in reserved sauerkraut liquid; cook and stir until thickened.
Cooked beef, cut into 1-inch cubes	3 1/2 quarts	5. Add reserved cracklings, sausage, mushrooms, sauerkraut, and remaining ingredients except wine. Cover and simmer for 30 minutes.
Cooked chicken or turkey, cut into pieces	2 1/4 quarts	
Cooked ham, cut into 1-inch pieces	2 1/4 quarts	
Onion flakes	2 cups	
Bay leaves	6	
Ground black pepper	1 1/2 teaspoons	
Sherry, Madeira, or dry red wine	3 cups	6. Stir in wine; simmer for 15 minutes longer.
		7. Garnish with parsley flakes and serve with boiled potatoes, if desired.

Hungarian Goulash

Yield: 48 portions

Featured Seasonings: onions, paprika, salt, ground black pepper, ground marjoram, dry white wine

Ingredients	Quantities	Procedure
Shortening, divided	1 1/2 cups	1. In a heavy sauce pot, heat 1 cup of the shortening until hot. Add onions; sauté until tender. Remove onions; set aside.
Onions, chopped	4 quarts	
Stew beef, boneless, cut into 1 1/2-inch cubes	20 pounds	2. Add remaining shortening to pot. Add meat (do not crowd); brown well on all sides.
Paprika	1 cup	3. Sprinkle meat with paprika, salt, black pepper, and marjoram. Stir in broth, wine, green pepper, and reserved sautéed onions. Bring to the boiling point. Reduce heat and simmer, covered, until meat is tender, about 2 hours.
Salt	1/4 cup	
Ground black pepper	2 teaspoons	
Ground marjoram	2 teaspoons	
Beef broth or water	5 quarts	4. Remove meat to a steam table pan.
Dry white wine	1 1/2 quarts	
Green peppers, diced	1 quart	
Flour	2 cups	5. Strain gravy. Mix flour with water. Gradually stir into gravy. Cook and stir until thickened. Pour over beef.
Water	1/2 cup	
		6. Serve with poppy seed noodles, if desired.

Svinge Kotlety s Sousom Gli Kislykh Vishen
(Breaded Pork Chops with Cherry Sauce)

Yield: 48 portions

Featured Seasonings: salt, ground black pepper, paprika, lemon juice, ground cinnamon, ground allspice, ground cloves, port wine

Ingredients	Quantities	Procedure
Flour	2 2/3 cups	1. Mix flour with 3 tablespoons salt and the black pepper.
Salt	As directed	
Ground black pepper	2 teaspoons	
Center cut pork chops, cut about		2. Dredge pork chops in flour mixture; shake off excess.
1/2-inch thick	48 (about 16 pounds)	
Eggs	8	3. Beat eggs with water.
Water	1 cup	
Fine dry bread crumbs	1 quart	4. Dip chops in egg; then coat in bread crumbs mixed with paprika.
Paprika	1/4 cup	
Salad oil	5 1/4 cups	5. Fry in oil preheated to 350°F. turning once until meat is fork tender, 20 to 25 minutes.
		6. Meanwhile, drain cherries; reserve juice. Set cherries aside.
Canned sour pitted cherries	8 (1 lb.) cans	7. Combine juice with sugar, cornstarch, lemon juice, spices, and 2 teaspoons salt. Bring to the boiling point, stirring constantly; cook and stir until thickened. Add reserved cherries and wine. Heat. Serve over pork chops.
Sugar	1 1/2 cups	
Cornstarch	1/2 cup	
Lemon juice	3 tablespoons	
Ground cinnamon	4 teaspoons	
Ground allspice	2 teaspoons	
Ground cloves	1 teaspoon	
Port wine	1 quart	

Vinha de Alhos (Azorian Style Pork Chops)

Yield: 48 portions

Featured Seasonings: salt, vinegar, garlic powder, ground red pepper, ground cumin seeds, ground cinnamon, ground cloves

Ingredients	Quantities	Procedure
Salt	3 tablespoons	1. Sprinkle salt over the bottom of large skillets. Heat until hot.
Pork chops, cut 3/4-inch thick	48 (about 14 pounds)	2. Add pork chops; brown on both sides, about 10 to 15 minutes.
		3. Remove chops from skillets.
		4. Remove skillets from heat; cool slightly.
Water	2 cups	5. Combine remaining ingredients; blend. Stir into skillets.
Vinegar	2 cups	6. Return to heat, stirring to loosen browned particles.
Flour	1/3 cup	7. Return chops to skillets; spoon sauce over chops.
Garlic powder	3 tablespoons	8. Simmer, covered, until tender, about 30 minutes.
Ground red pepper	1 tablespoon	9. Serve with steamed rice, if desired.
Ground cumin seeds	2 teaspoons	
Ground cinnamon	1/2 teaspoon	
Ground cloves	1/2 teaspoon	

Choucroute

Yield: 48 portions

Featured Seasonings: onions, garlic, dry white wine, bay leaves, juniper berries, whole black peppercorns, parsley flakes, caraway seeds, thyme leaves, salt

Ingredients	Quantities	Procedure
Bacon fat	1 1/2 cups	1. In large sauce pots, heat bacon fat. Add onions, carrots, and garlic. Cook over low heat until tender.
Onions, chopped	2 quarts	
Carrots, thinly sliced	2 quarts	
Garlic, minced	2 tablespoons	
Green apples, cored and diced	3 quarts	2. Add apples; cook 3 minutes longer.
Sauerkraut, rinsed and drained	16 pounds	3. Stir in sauerkraut, broth, and wine.
Chicken broth	1 gallon	
Dry white wine	1 1/2 quarts	
Bay leaves	8	4. Tie bay leaves, juniper berries, and peppercorns in a cheesecloth bag, and add to casserole along with parsley, caraway, and thyme.
Juniper berries	2 tablespoons	
Whole black peppercorns	1 teaspoon	
Parsley flakes, chopped	1 cup	5. Cover and cook for 15 minutes.
Caraway seeds	1/2 cup	
Thyme leaves	1 tablespoon	
Salt	2 teaspoons	6. Meanwhile, sprinkle salt in the bottom of a large skillet; heat until hot.
Pork chops	12 pounds	7. Add pork chops a few at a time and brown well on both sides.
		8. Remove chops and bury them in the sauerkraut.
Sausage	4 pounds	9. Brown sausage in the same skillet and add to casserole.
		10. Cover and bake in a preheated 325°F. oven until meat is tender, about 1 1/2 hours.

Pork Chops Charcutiere
(with Green Peppercorns)

Yield: 48 portions

Featured Seasonings: green peppercorns, salt, onions, tomato paste, dry sherry, garlic

Ingredients	Quantities	Procedure
Green peppercorns, undrained	1/3 cup	1. Crush peppercorns with a spoon or in a mortar with a pestle; set aside.
Loin pork chops, cut 1-inch thick	48 (16 pounds)	2. Sprinkle both sides of pork chops with salt.
Salt	2 tablespoons	
Bacon fat or oil	1/2 cup	3. In large skillets, heat fat until hot. Add the chops a few at a time; brown well on both sides. Add water. Simmer, covered, until meat is tender, about 40 minutes, turning occasionally.
Water	1 1/2 cups	
Butter or margarine	1 cup	4. In a sauce pan, melt butter. Add onions and garlic; sauté until golden brown. Stir in flour. Gradually blend in broth. Stir in reserved peppercorns along with remaining ingredients. Cook over low heat for 15 minutes, stirring occasionally.
Onions, chopped	1 quart	
Garlic, minced	4 teaspoons	
Flour	3/4 cup	
Beef broth	3 quarts	5. Remove chops to warm serving dishes; set aside.
Dill pickle, chopped	2 2/3 cups	6. Drain off fat in skillet. Add gravy to pan and heat, stirring to loosen browned particles. Pour over chops and serve.
Tomato paste	1/2 cup	
Dry sherry	1/2 cup	

Braised Pork Chops in Dill and Paprika Sauce

Yield: 48 portions

Featured Seasonings: onions, paprika, dill seeds, salt, ground black pepper, garlic powder, sour cream

Ingredients	Quantities	Procedure
Pork chops, cut about 1-inch thick	48 (16 pounds)	1. Dredge pork chops lightly with flour.
Flour	As needed	
Oil	1 1/2 cups	2. In a large, heavy skillet, heat oil until hot. Add chops, a few at a time; cook until golden brown on both sides. Remove and set aside.
Onions, minced	2 quarts	3. To oil left in pan, add onions; sauté until golden brown.
Chicken broth	2 quarts	4. Stir in chicken broth, paprika, dill seeds, salt, black pepper, and garlic powder.
Paprika	1 cup	
Dill seeds	1/3 cup	5. Return pork to skillet; spoon sauce over chops.
Salt	2 tablespoons	6. Cover tightly and simmer until pork is tender, about 1 hour. Remove chops and keep warm.
Ground black pepper	1 teaspoon	
Garlic powder	1 teaspoon	
Heavy cream	1 quart	7. Add heavy cream and sour cream to skillet. Stir and simmer gently until sauce is lightly thickened. Serve with noodles or spatzle, if desired.
Sour cream, dairy	1 quart	

Shahi Kofta (Ground Lamb Kebabs)

Featured Seasonings: whole saffron, salt, ground coriander, ground cumin seeds, ground ginger, ground cardamom, ground cinnamon, ground black pepper, cloves, onions, lemon juice

Ingredients	Quantities	Procedure
Whole saffron	1 tablespoon	1. Crumble saffron in boiling water; set aside.
Boiling water	3/4 cup	
Flour	As needed	2. In a large mixing bowl, combine 1 1/2 cups flour with egg, salt, and spices. Stir in lamb.
Eggs, lightly beaten	12	
Salt	1/4 cup	
Ground coriander	3/4 cup	
Ground cumin seeds	1/4 cup	
Ground ginger	2 tablespoons	
Ground cardamom	2 tablespoons	
Ground cinnamon	1 tablespoon	
Ground black pepper	1 tablespoon	
Cloves	1 1/2 teaspoons	
Ground lean lamb	12 pounds	
Lemon juice	1 1/2 cups	3. Add lemon juice, yogurt, reserved saffron mixture, and onions; mix well, but do not overmix.
Plain yogurt	1 1/2 cups	
Onions, minced	1 quart	4. Shape into sausage-like cylinders about 2-inches long by 1-inch wide.
		5. Roll in flour; shake off excess.
Oil, salad	As needed	6. In a large skillet heat a thin coating of oil. Add meat rolls, a few at a time, and brown evenly, turning frequently, about 5 minutes. Add additional oil as needed.
		7. Arrange on skewers and serve with sliced tomatoes and lemon wedges, if desired.

Note: Lamb also may be skewered and broiled under a preheated broiler or over hot charcoal, if desired.

Sfeeha (Syrian Peppery Lamb Pies)

Yield: 60 meat pies

Featured Seasonings: onions, olive oil, lemon juice, parsley, tomato paste, salt, ground allspice, ground red pepper, sesame seed

Ingredients	Quantities	Procedure
Prepared yeast bread dough	10 pounds (using 16–20 cups flour	1. Shape dough into a ball and place in a buttered bowl; cover and let rise until double in bulk, 45 to 60 minutes.
		2. Punch down dough; divide into 60 equal parts.
		3. Shape each part into a ball; cover and let rest for 30 minutes.
Olive oil	2 tablespoons	4. In a small skillet, heat oil. Add pine nuts; sauté until golden; set aside.
Pine nuts	1 cup	
Onions, minced	2 cups	5. In a large bowl combine onions, green peppers, tomatoes, parsley, lemon juice, tomato paste, salt, allspice, red pepper, and lamb; blend well.
Green peppers, chopped	1/2 cup	
Tomatoes, peeled, seeded, and finely diced	1 1/2 pounds	6. On a lightly floured board, roll each of the balls into a 5-inch round, 1/8-inch thick.
Parsley, chopped	1/2 cup	
Lemon juice	1 cup	7. Place approximately 1/3-cup lamb mixture on each round. Bring edges of dough together over the filling. Pinch together along sides to form three corners.
Tomato paste	1/4 cup	
Salt	4 teaspoons	
Ground allspice	2 1/2 teaspoons	
Ground red pepper	1 teaspoon	
Ground lean lamb	4 pounds	
Egg wash	As needed	8. Place on greased baking sheets. Brush with egg wash. Sprinkle with sesame seeds.
Sesame seeds	As needed	
		9. Bake in a preheated 425°F. oven until lightly browned, 18 to 20 minutes.
		10. Serve hot or at room temperature.

English Shepherd's Pie

Yield: 48 portions

Featured Seasonings: onions, garlic, carrots, tomato paste, parsley, bay leaves, salt, sage leaves, thyme leaves, ground black pepper, cheddar cheese

Ingredients	Quantities	Procedure
Oil, salad	1 cup	1. In a large skillet, heat oil until hot. Add onions and garlic; sauté until tender; remove from skillet.
Onions, minced	2 cups	
Garlic, minced	3 tablespoons	
Ground lean beef	12 pounds	2. Add beef; cook and stir until browned. Return onions and garlic to skillet.
		3. Stir in flour; cook and stir for 2 minutes. Stir in beef broth.
Flour	1 cup	
Beef broth	1 1/2 quarts	
Carrots, diced	2 quarts	4. Add carrots, tomato paste, parsley, bay leaves, salt, sage, thyme, and black pepper; mix well. Bring to the boiling point.
Tomato paste	1 1/2 cups	
Parsley, chopped	1 cup	5. Reduce heat and simmer, covered, until carrots are tender, about 10 minutes. Remove bay leaves. Pour into individual casseroles.
Bay leaves	8	
Salt	3 tablespoons	
Sage leaves, crumbled	4 teaspoons	
Thyme leaves, crumbled	2 teaspoons	
Ground black pepper	2 teaspoons	
Mashed potatoes, seasoned	1 1/2 gallons	6. Top with mashed potatoes; spread smooth. Mark top of potato with tines of a fork.
Cheddar cheese, shredded	2 cups	7. Sprinkle with cheese.
		8. Bake in a preheated 375 °F. oven until hot and golden, about 15 minutes.

Cannelloni

Yield: 48 portions

Featured Seasonings: onions, garlic, parmesan cheese, marjoram leaves, salt, ground black pepper

Ingredients	Quantities	Procedure
Oil, olive	1 1/2 cups	1. In a large skillet, heat oil. Add onions and garlic; sauté until tender. Add beef and mushrooms. Cook until meat is brown.
Onions, minced	2 quarts	
Garlic, minced	4 teaspoons	
Ground lean beef	8 pounds	
Canned mushroom stems and pieces, drained	8 (6 to 8 oz.) cans	
Frozen chopped spinach, thawed	8 (10 oz.) packages	2. Squeeze as much liquid as possible from spinach. Add to meat mixture.
		3. Sauté over high heat, stirring constantly, until mixture begins to stick to pan. Turn into a mixing bowl.
Parmesan cheese, grated	2 2/3 cups	4. Add parmesan cheese, eggs, cream, marjoram, salt, and black pepper; mix well.
Eggs, beaten	16	
Heavy or light cream	1 cup	
Marjoram leaves, crumbled	2 tablespoons	
Salt	2 tablespoons	
Ground black pepper	1 teaspoon	
Prepared crepes	96	5. Spoon filling onto each crepe; roll up.
Medium white sauce	2 quarts	6. In the bottom of two large shallow baking pans, pour half the white sauce. Then pour half the spaghetti sauce over the white sauce.
Spaghetti sauce	1 1/4 gallons	
		7. Place filled crepes seam side down over sauces, side by side. Pour remaining spaghetti sauce over all.
		8. Bake, uncovered, in a preheated 375°F. oven until hot, 20 to 30 minutes. Serve at once.

Konigsberger Klopse (Meatballs in Lemon Sauce)

Yield: 48 portions

Featured Seasonings: onions, anchovy fillets, parsley, lemon peel, ground ginger, salt, ground black pepper, bay leaves, whole cloves, capers, lemon juice, sour cream

Ingredients	Quantities	Procedure
Onions, minced, divided	1 1/2 quarts	1. In a large mixing bowl, combine 3 cups of the bread crumbs, onions, milk, eggs, anchovies, parsley, half of the lemon peel, ginger, 3 tablespoons salt, and black pepper.
Water	4 gallons	
Soft bread crumbs	3 quarts	
Milk	2 2/3 cups	
Eggs, beaten	16	
Anchovy fillets, crushed	24	
Parsley, chopped	2 cups	
Lemon peel, grated, divided	1/3 cup	
Ground ginger	4 teaspoons	
Salt, divided	4 tablespoons	
Ground black pepper	2 teaspoons	
Ground beef	4 pounds	2. Add meat; mix well.
Ground pork	4 pounds	
Ground veal	4 pounds	
Flour	As needed	3. Shape into 2-inch balls. Roll in flour, shake off excess; set aside.
Bay leaves	8	4. In a large sauce pan combine water, remaining 3 cups minced onion, and 1 tablespoon salt. Add bay leaves and cloves. Bring to the boiling point. Boil rapidly for 10 minutes.
Whole cloves	16	
		5. Add meatballs. Return to the boiling point. Reduce heat and simmer, uncovered, for 20 minutes. Remove meatballs; keep warm.
		6. Strain and reserve 5 quarts broth used to cook meatballs.
Butter or margarine	1 pound	7. In a sauce pan melt butter. Stir in 2 cups flour; cook 2 minutes.

99

(continued on next page)

Konigsberger Klopse (cont'd.)

Ingredients	Quantities	Procedure
Egg yolks, beaten	16	Gradually add reserved broth; cook and stir until smooth, about 2 minutes. Add some hot sauce to egg yolks; then stir into remaining sauce in sauce pan. Add capers, lemon juice, and remaining lemon peel; cook until smooth and thick, stirring often. Stir in sour cream. Heat until hot. DO NOT BOIL.
Capers, drained	1/3 cup	
Lemon juice	1/2 cup	
Sour cream, dairy	2 cups	
		8. Season with salt and white pepper to taste, if needed. Spoon over meatballs.

Crispy Onion Steaks

Yield: 48 portions

Featured Seasonings: salt, ground black pepper, sliced onions

Ingredients	Quantities	Procedure
Flour	1 1/2 quarts	1. Combine flour with salt and black pepper.
Salt	3 tablespoons	
Ground black pepper	1 teaspoon	
Eggs, lightly beaten	6	2. Mix eggs with milk.
Milk	1 quart	
Beef top round steaks, cut 1/4-inch thick	48 pieces (about 12 pounds)	3. Coat both sides of meat, first with seasoned flour; then dip in egg mixture and then in sliced onion, pressing to make sure onion adheres well to meat.
Instant sliced onion	1 1/2 quarts	
Oil, salad	As needed	4. Pour oil to depth of 1/4 inch into large skillets; heat until hot.
		5. Add steaks to skillets; brown lightly on both sides, adding oil as needed.
		6. If desired, serve with mustard brown sauce. Fish fillets, chicken, turkey, or veal cutlets can be prepared the same way.

Cornish Pasties

Yield: 48 portions

Featured Seasonings: onion, parsley flakes, salt, ground black pepper, ground ginger

Ingredients	Quantities	Procedure
Pastry	8 pounds	1. Divide pastry into 48 parts. Roll each part into a 7-inch round.
Ground lean beef	6 pounds	2. Combine remaining ingredients, except milk.
Cooked potatoes, diced	3 quarts	3. Place about 1/2 cup of meat mixture on one side of each round.
Instant minced onion	1/3 cup	
Parsley flakes	1/3 cup	
Salt	2 tablespoons	
Ground black pepper	1 1/2 teaspoons	
Ground ginger	1 1/2 teaspoons	
Milk	As needed	4. Moisten edges of dough with water; fold dough over filling and press edges firmly together. Cut slits on top of each turnover. Brush with milk. Place on ungreased baking sheets.
		5. Bake in a preheated 400 °F. oven for 15 minutes. Reduce heat to 350 °F. and bake until crust is brown, 35 to 40 minutes.
		6. Serve hot or cold.

Hamburger Heavenly Hash

Yield: 50 portions

Featured Seasonings: onions, garlic, soy sauce, chili powder, dry mustard, salt

Ingredients	Quantities	Procedure
Ground beef	8 pounds	1. Brown beef with onions and garlic. Add cooking oil if necessary. Add soy sauce, chili powder, mustard, tomatoes, water, and salt to meat. Heat to the boiling point.
Onions, chopped	1 1/2 quarts	
Garlic, minced	2 tablespoons	
Soy sauce	1 1/2 cups	
Chili powder	1/4 cup	
Powdered mustard	1 1/2 tablespoons	
Canned tomatoes	1 1/2 (No. 10) cans	
Water	2 quarts	
Salt	1 tablespoon	
Elbow macaroni, uncooked	3 pounds	2. Divide uncooked elbow macaroni into pans, using 2 pounds in each pan.
Green peppers, chopped	1 quart	3. Sprinkle green peppers on top of macaroni.
		4. Pour hot meat sauce mixture into pans over macaroni and stir for 1 minute.
		5. Cover and bake in a preheated 400°F. oven for about 20 minutes.
Cheddar or processed cheese, grated	1 pound	6. Uncover; stir. Sprinkle with cheese. Return to oven to melt cheese. Serve hot.

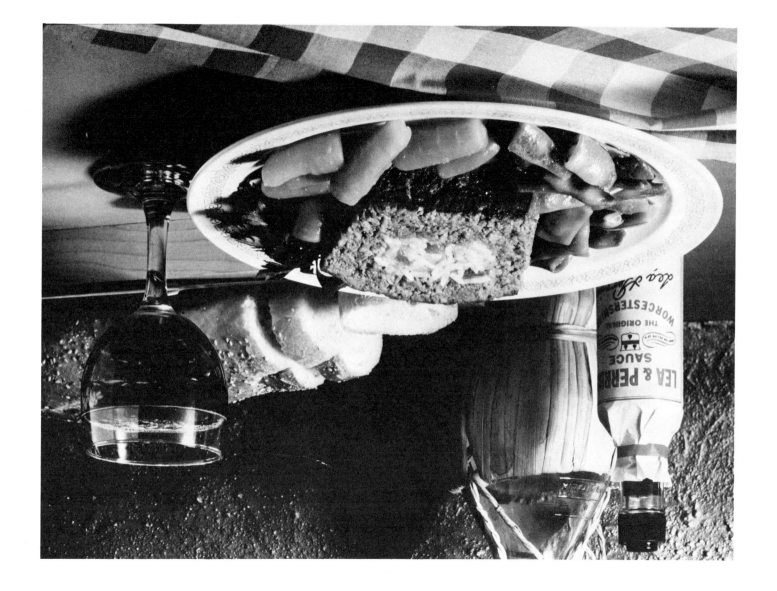

Italian Stuffed Meat Loaf

Yield: 48 portions

Featured Seasonings: onions, tomato sauce, Worcestershire sauce, salt, ground black pepper, green peppers, cheddar cheese, Italian seasoning, garlic powder

Ingredients	Quantities	Procedure
Ground beef	16 pounds	1. Combine beef, bread crumbs, 1 1/2 quarts of the onions, tomato sauce, 8 of the eggs, 1/3 cup of the Worcestershire sauce, 3 tablespoons of the salt, and the black pepper. Mix well, but do not overmix.
Soft bread crumbs	1 quart	
Onions, finely chopped, divided	2 quarts	
Tomato sauce	2 quarts	
Eggs, divided	12	2. Divide meat mixture into 8 portions.
Worcestershire sauce	1/3 cup	3. Place 3/4 of each portion in a 9 x 5 x 3-inch loaf pan; pat gently to fit bottom and sides of pans, making a well in the center.
Salt, divided	3 tablespoons	
Ground black pepper	1 teaspoon	
Butter or margarine	1/2 cup	4. In a skillet, heat butter. Add remaining 2 cups onions and green peppers; sauté until tender.
Green peppers, chopped	1 cup	
Cooked rice	1 3/4 quarts	5. Stir in rice. Add remaining 4 eggs, 1/3 cup Worcestershire sauce, chopped tomatoes, cheddar cheese, green olives, Italian seasoning, garlic powder, and 1 1/2 tablespoons salt; mix well.
Tomatoes, chopped	3/4 quart	
Cheddar cheese, grated	2 cups	
Pitted green olives, chopped	1/2 cup	6. Spoon rice mixture into well of each meatloaf.
Italian seasoning	2 teaspoons	7. Top with remaining reserved meat.
Garlic powder	1 teaspoon	8. Bake in a preheated 350°F. oven for 1 1/2 hours or until firm.
		9. Let rest in pans 10 minutes before turning out. Slice and serve.

Frikkadela (South African Meat Patties)

Yield: 48 portions

Featured Seasonings: onion powder, salt, ground coriander, ground nutmeg, ground black pepper

Ingredients	Quantities	Procedure
Ground beef	6 pounds	1. In a large bowl, combine beef, lamb, bread crumbs, eggs, onion powder, salt, coriander, nutmeg, black pepper, and 1 1/2 cups of the beef broth. Shape into patties, 2 inches in diameter.
Ground lamb	6 pounds	
Soft bread crumbs	1 1/2 quarts	
Eggs, lightly beaten	12	
Onion powder	1/3 cup	
Salt	1/4 cup	
Ground coriander	2 tablespoons	
Ground nutmeg	1 1/2 teaspoons	
Ground black pepper	1 1/2 teaspoons	
Canned condensed beef broth, divided	1 (50 oz.) can	
Oil, peanut	3/4 cup	2. In a large skillet, heat oil until hot. Add patties, a few at a time, brown on both sides; remove and set aside.
		3. Stir remaining beef broth into drippings in skillet, stirring well to scrape drippings from bottom of pan.
		4. Return patties to skillet. Bring to the boiling point. Reduce heat and simmer, covered, until patties are cooked, about 15 minutes.
		5. Remove patties to a serving container; keep warm.
Flour	1/3 cup	6. Blend flour with water. Mix into liquid in skillet. Cook and stir until mixture boils and thickens; spoon over patties.
Cold water	1/3 cup	7. If desired, surround with saffron rice with raisins.

Dolmasi (Stuffed Eggplant)

Yield: 48 portions

Featured Seasonings: olive oil, onions, garlic, tomato sauce, parsley, mint flakes, dill seeds, salt, ground black pepper, toasted sesame seeds

Ingredients	Quantities	Procedure
Eggplants, medium sized	24	1. Slice eggplants in half lengthwise; cut out pulp, leaving a 1-inch thick shell. Reserve pulp and shells.
Olive oil	1/2 cup	2. In a large sauce pot, heat oil until hot. Add onions and garlic; sauté until tender.
Onions, chopped	2 quarts	
Garlic, minced	2 tablespoons	
Ground lean lamb	8 pounds	3. Add lamb; cook until meat is brown. Drain off excess fat.
		4. Coarsely chop eggplant pulp and add to meat mixture.
Tomato sauce	1 (No. 10) can	5. Stir in tomato sauce and water; cook 10 minutes, stirring occasionally.
Water	5 cups	
Quick-cooking rice	1 1/2 quarts	6. Remove from heat; add rice, parsley, mint flakes, dill seed, salt, and black pepper; mix well.
Parsley, chopped	1 cup	
Mint flakes, crumbled	1 tablespoon	
Dill seeds	1 tablespoon	
Salt	1 tablespoon	
Ground black pepper	2 teaspoons	
Sesame seeds, toasted	2 cups	7. Fill eggplant shells with the stuffing. Sprinkle tops with sesame seeds. Arrange shells in a buttered baking pan. Add 1/4-inch boiling water to baking pan.
Water, boiling	As directed	
Tomatoes, sliced	8	8. Cover and bake in a preheated 350°F. oven until eggplant is tender, about 1 hour.
		9. Place 1 tomato slice on top of each eggplant. Place under broiler for a few seconds just to heat tomato. Serve.

Picadinho (Meat Hash)

Yield: 48 portions

Featured Seasonings: onions, oregano leaves, salt, ground red pepper

Ingredients	Quantities	Procedure
Olive or salad oil	1/2 cup	1. Heat oil in large skillets.
Ground beef	12 pounds	2. Add beef and onions; sauté until meat is well browned.
Onions, minced	1 quart	
Tomatoes, chopped	1 gallon	3. Add tomatoes, oregano, salt, and red pepper.
Oregano leaves	2 tablespoons	
Salt	2 tablespoons	
Ground red pepper	2 teaspoons	
Beef broth	2 to 4 cups	4. Stir in broth. Cover and simmer for 30 minutes.
Medium-sized potatoes, boiled, peeled, and diced	8	5. Just before serving, stir in potatoes and olives; top with eggs. Serve with rice.
Stuffed olives, sliced	2 cups	
Hard-cooked eggs, sliced	16	
Hot steamed rice	As needed	

Onion Meat Loaf

Featured Seasonings: onions, powdered mustard, salt, garlic powder, ground black pepper, Worcestershire sauce

Ingredients	Quantities	Procedure
Dry bread crumbs	1 quart	1. In a large bowl combine bread crumbs, onion, mustard, salt, garlic powder, black pepper, tomato juice, eggs, and Worcestershire sauce.
Instant chopped onion	2 cups	
Powdered mustard	1 tablespoon	
Salt	1/4 cup	
Garlic powder	2 tablespoons	
Ground black pepper	1 1/2 teaspoons	
Tomato juice	1 quart	
Eggs, beaten	6	
Worcestershire sauce	1/4 cup	
Ground beef	9 pounds	2. Add meat; combine but do not overmix.
Ground veal	1 1/2 pounds	3. Shape meat into 8 loaves, 1 1/2 pounds each. Place on lightly oiled roasting pans.
Ground pork	1 1/2 pounds	4. Bake in a preheated 350°F. oven for 1 hour. Remove from oven. Let rest 20 minutes before slicing.

Veal with Green Peppercorns

Yield: 48 portions

Featured Seasonings: green peppercorns, salt, butter, dry white wine, parsley

Ingredients	Quantities	Procedure
Green peppercorns, undrained	3 tablespoons	1. Crush peppercorns with a spoon or in a mortar with a pestle; set aside.
Veal, thinly sliced	12 pounds	2. Place each piece of veal between waxed paper; pound lightly until thin.
Salt	1/4 cup	3. Sprinkle both sides of meat with salt. Dredge with flour; shake off excess.
Flour	As needed	
Butter or margarine	1 pound	4. In a large skillet, melt 1/8 of the butter at a time. Add veal, a few pieces at a time, and brown quickly over moderately high heat. Remove meat from skillet. Keep warm. Continue adding more butter and veal until all meat is browned.
Water or chicken broth	1 1/2 cups	5. Add water to skillet; stir to loosen browned particles.
Dry white wine	1 1/2 cups	6. Add wine and reserved peppercorns. Heat for 1 minute.
Parsley, finely chopped	1/3 cup	7. Pour over veal. Sprinkle with parsley. Serve with lemon slices, if desired.

POULTRY

Coq a la Mode de Cluny
(Chicken, Ham, and Cabbage Stew)

Yield: 48 to 72 portions

Featured Seasonings: shallots, onions, garlic, white burgundy wine, parsley, basil leaves, thyme leaves, ground black pepper

Ingredients	Quantities	Procedure
Bacon strips	1 1/2 pounds	1. In a large sauce pot, fry bacon until crisp. Remove bacon; crumble and set aside.
Chicken parts	30 pounds	2. Add chicken; brown well on both sides. Remove chicken when browned; set aside.
Butter or margarine	1 1/2 cups	3. Melt butter in skillet. Add mushrooms, onions, shallots, and garlic; sauté until tender. Remove half of the mushroom mixture to baking pans. Lay cabbage over mushroom mixture in baking pans. Place chicken over cabbage. Add ham.
Mushrooms, sliced	3 pounds	
Onions, chopped	1 1/2 quarts	
Shallots, chopped	3 cups	
Garlic, minced	3 tablespoons	
Cabbages, cut into wedges	12 small	
Ham	9 pounds	
Chicken broth	3 quarts	4. Combine chicken broth, wine, parsley, salt, basil, thyme, black pepper, and reserved bacon. Pour over all.
White burgundy wine	1 quart	
Parsley, chopped	1 3/4 cups	5. Top with reserved mushroom mixture.
Basil leaves, crumbled	2 tablespoons	6. Cover and bake in a preheated 350°F. oven until chicken is tender, about 30 to 40 minutes.
Thyme leaves, crumbled	1 tablespoon	
Ground black pepper	1 1/2 teaspoons	

Groundnut Stew

Yield: 48 portions

Featured Seasonings: salt, onions, garlic, tomato paste, ground ginger, ground red pepper

Ingredients	Quantities	Procedure
Chicken parts	30 pounds	1. Sprinkle chicken with 5 tablespoons of the salt.
Salt, divided	9 tablespoons	
Peanut oil	1 1/2 cups	2. In a large sauce pot, heat oil until hot. Add chicken, a few pieces at a time; brown well. Remove chicken as it browns.
Onions, chopped	3 cups	3. After chicken is browned add onions, green peppers, and garlic; sauté until tender.
Green peppers, chopped	2 cups	
Garlic, minced	1 1/2 tablespoons	
Tomato paste	3 (12 oz.) cans	4. Stir in tomato paste, ginger, red pepper, and remaining 4 tablespoons salt. Stir in 3 quarts of the boiling water; blend well.
Ground ginger	1/4 cup	
Ground red pepper	1 tablespoon	5. Return chicken to sauce pot. Simmer, covered, until chicken is almost tender, about 30 minutes.
Boiling water, divided	1 gallon	
Chunk style peanut butter	1 1/2 quarts	6. Mix peanut butter with remaining 1 quart boiling water. Stir into sauce pot. Add shrimp, eggplant, and okra. Simmer until shrimp, vegetables, and chicken are tender, 15 to 20 minutes.
Raw shrimp, peeled and deveined	3 pounds	
Eggplant, diced	3 quarts	
Okra	3 pounds	

Arroz con Pollo (Chicken with Rice)

Yield: 48 portions

Featured Seasonings: olive oil, onions, green peppers, garlic, salt, oregano leaves, paprika, ground black pepper, saffron

Ingredients	Quantities	Procedure
Olive oil	2 2/3 cups	1. In a large sauce pot, heat oil until hot. Add chicken; brown on all sides; remove.
Chicken parts	20 pounds	
Onions, minced	2 quarts	2. Add onions, green peppers and garlic; sauté until tender. Return chicken to pot. Add seasonings, tomatoes, ham, and olives. Cover and simmer for 10 minutes.
Green peppers, chopped	1 quart	
Garlic, minced	1 tablespoon	
Salt	1/3 cup	
Oregano leaves	2 1/2 teaspoons	
Paprika	2 tablespoons	
Ground black pepper	1 tablespoon	
Crushed tomatoes	2 (No. 10) cans	
Smoked ham, chopped	1 quart	
Green olives, sliced	2 cups	
Boiling water	1 1/2 gallons	3. Add boiling water, rice, and saffron; stir gently. Cover and continue simmering until chicken is tender, 25 to 30 minutes longer.
Regular cooking raw rice	2 quarts	
Saffron	2 teaspoons	
Cooked frozen peas	2 (40 oz.) packages	4. Add peas to chicken. Serve hot with pimiento strips, if desired.

Caribbean Chicken and Rice

Yield: 48 portions

Featured Seasonings: onions, garlic, salt, ground red pepper, coconut milk, whole cloves, ground cinnamon

Ingredients	Quantities	Procedure
Oil, salad	1 cup	1. In a heavy sauce pot, heat oil until hot. Add chicken (do not crowd); brown well on all sides. Remove chicken and all but 1/2 cup oil.
Chicken parts	40 pounds	
Onions, minced	3 cups	2. Add onions and garlic; sauté until lightly browned.
Garlic, minced	2 tablespoons	
Salt	1/3 cup	3. Return chicken to sauce pot. Sprinkle with salt and red pepper. Add water. Cover and simmer until chicken is almost tender, about 20 minutes.
Ground red pepper	2 teaspoons	
Water	1 gallon	
Coconut milk*	2 quarts	4. Add remaining ingredients, including coconut milk. Simmer, covered, until chicken and rice are tender, about 20 minutes.
Raw regular cooking rice	2 quarts	
Whole cloves	1 1/2 teaspoons	
Ground cinnamon	1 tablespoon	

*To make coconut milk, combine 2 pounds shredded coconut with 3 quarts water or milk in sauce pan. Bring to the boiling point, simmer 10 minutes. Strain, reserving liquid.

Chicken Livers and Rice, Portuguese Style

Yield: 48 portions

Featured Seasonings: onions, garlic, olive oil, bay leaves, ground white pepper, salt, parsley

Ingredients	Quantities	Procedure
Olive oil	1 1/2 cups	1. In a large skillet, heat oil and butter. Add onions, garlic, and bay leaves; sauté for 5 minutes, stirring. Remove and discard bay leaves.
Butter or margarine	1 1/2 cups	
Garlic, minced	1/4 cup	
Onions, chopped	2 quarts	
Bay leaves, small	12	
Chicken livers, halved	12 pounds	2. Add chicken livers, paprika, and water. Cook, covered, over low heat for 10 minutes. Remove chicken livers; set aside.
Paprika	2 tablespoons	
Water	1/2 cup	
Rich chicken broth	6 quarts	3. In a sauce pot, bring broth to the boiling point. Season with white pepper and salt to taste. Stir in rice and parsley. Simmer, covered, until rice is tender, about 20 minutes. Stir in reserved livers. Heat until hot.
Ground white pepper	1 teaspoon	
Salt	As needed (to taste)	
Raw regular cooking rice	3 quarts	
Parsley, chopped	1 1/2 cups	

Matok V' Hamutz Tarnegoal
(Stewed Chicken and Meatballs, Israeli Style)

Yield: 48 portions

Featured Seasonings: salt, ground black pepper, onion powder, garlic powder, onions, garlic, paprika, lemon juice

Ingredients	Quantities	Procedure
Chicken parts	20 pounds	1. Sprinkle chicken with 2 tablespoons of the salt and 1 teaspoon of the black pepper; set aside for 1 hour.
Salt, divided	3 tablespoons	
Ground black pepper, divided	2 teaspoons	
Ground lean beef	8 pounds	2. In a small mixing bowl, combine beef, bread crumbs, onion and garlic powders, the remaining 1 tablespoon salt, and 1 teaspoon black pepper. Mix well, but do not overmix. Shape into 1-inch meatballs; set aside.
Soft bread crumbs	2 cups	
Onion powder	1/4 cup	
Garlic powder	1 teaspoon	
Oil, salad	1/2 cup	3. In a large sauce pot, heat oil until hot. Add chicken, a few pieces at a time; brown well. Remove chicken; set aside.
		4. Add meatballs and brown. Remove meatballs; set aside.
Onions, minced	2 quarts	5. Add onion and garlic to sauce pot; sauté until tender. Stir in flour and paprika; cook and stir for 1 minute.
Garlic, minced	1 tablespoon	
Flour	1 cup	
Paprika	1/2 cup	
Chicken broth	3 quarts	6. Stir in chicken broth, lemon juice, and brown sugar. Return chicken and meatballs to sauce pot. Simmer, covered, until chicken is tender, about 45 minutes. Garnish with parsley.
Lemon juice	1 cup	
Brown sugar, firmly packed	1 cup	

Spicy Szechuan Chicken and Walnuts

Yield: 48 portions

Featured Seasonings: salt, onions, garlic, sesame seeds or salad oil, crushed Szechuan or cracked black pepper, ground ginger, soy sauce, sweet sherry

Ingredients	Quantities	Procedure
Chicken breasts, skinned, boned and halved	24	1. Cut chicken into 1-inch cubes.
Egg whites, lightly beaten	16	2. In a medium bowl combine egg whites, 2 cups of the cornstarch, and salt.
Cornstarch, divided	2 1/2 cups	
Salt	2 teaspoons	3. Dip chicken pieces into egg mixture.
Oil or fat for deep frying	as needed	4. Drop a few pieces at a time into oil preheated to 375°F. Fry until chicken is golden and fork tender, about 5 minutes. Drain on paper towels; keep warm.
Onions, minced	1 cup	
Garlic, minced	2 teaspoons	
Cold water	1 cup	
Sesame seeds or salad oil	1 cup	5. In a skillet heat oil until hot. Add onion, garlic, pepper, and ginger; saute for 2 minutes. Add walnuts; sauté for 1 minute longer.
Szechuan pepper, crushed or cracked black pepper	2 tablespoons Szechuan pepper or 4 teaspoons cracked black pepper	
		6. Dissolve bouillon cubes in boiling water. Blend the remaining cornstarch with soy sauce; stir in chicken bouillon.
Ground ginger	4 teaspoons	
Walnut halves	2 quarts	
Chicken bouillon cubes	8	
Boiling water	2 1/2 quarts	
Soy sauce	1 cup	
Sweet sherry	1 cup	7. Blend into onion mixture in skillet along with sherry and sugar. Cook and stir over low heat until thickened.
Sugar	2 tablespoons	
		8. Pour over crispy fried chicken pieces.

Chili Chicken

Yield: 48 portions

Featured Seasonings: onions, salt, garlic, chili powder

Ingredients	Quantities	Procedure
Chicken quarters	35 pounds	1. Place chicken into a large sauce pot. Cover with water. Bring to the boiling point. Add onions, salt, and garlic. Reduce heat and simmer, covered, until chicken is tender, about 30 minutes. Remove chicken; cool. Reserve broth.
Onions, minced	1 quart	
Salt	2/3 cup	
Garlic, minced	3 tablespoons	
Tomatoes, crushed	1 (No. 10) can	2. Remove skin from chicken and take meat off the bones. Strain chicken broth, reserving 1 gallon. Return meat and broth to sauce pot. Add tomatoes, corn, and chili powder. Simmer, covered, 30 minutes longer.
Corn kernels	1 (No. 10) can	
Chili powder	1/4 cup	3. Serve hot with corn bread, if desired.

Ethiopian Chicken

Yield: 48 portions

Featured Seasonings: onions, garlic, spiced butter, paprika, ground ginger, ground nutmeg, ground coriander, ground red pepper, ground black pepper, dry white wine, salt, lemon juice

Ingredients	Quantities	Procedure
Spiced Butter (see following recipe)	3 cups	1. In a large skillet, melt Spiced Butter. Add onions and garlic; sauté until tender.
Onions, chopped	2 1/4 quarts	
Garlic, minced	1/3 cup	
Paprika	1 cup	2. Add paprika, ginger, nutmeg, coriander, and red and black peppers. Cook and stir for 1 minute.
Ground ginger	1 1/2 teaspoons	
Ground nutmeg	1 1/2 teaspoons	
Ground coriander	1 1/2 teaspoons	
Ground red pepper	1 1/2 teaspoons	
Ground black pepper	1 1/2 teaspoons	
Water	1 1/2 quarts	3. Add water and wine; bring to the boiling point. Reduce heat and simmer, uncovered, for 10 minutes.
Dry white wine	3 cups	
Chicken parts	35 pounds	4. Meanwhile, sprinkle chicken with salt and lemon juice; let stand for 10 minutes. Add chicken to sauce in skillet.
Salt	1/4 cup	
Lemon juice	3/4 cup	5. Simmer, covered, for 30 minutes, stirring and spooning sauce over chicken occasionally.
Hard-cooked eggs	48	6. Add eggs, spooning some sauce over eggs. Cover and simmer for 15 minutes longer.
		7. Remove chicken and eggs. Reduce sauce in skillet to half. Spoon over chicken and eggs. Serve immediately, over hot, fluffy rice if desired.

Spiced Butter (for Ethiopian Chicken)

Yield:	3 cups
Featured Seasonings:	onion, stick cinnamon, garlic, ginger root, whole cloves, whole cardamom pods, ground turmeric

Ingredients	Quantities	Procedure
Butter	1 1/2 pounds	1. In a medium saucepan, melt butter. Add remaining ingredients. Cook over low heat for 30 minutes, stirring occasionally.
Chopped onion	3 tablespoons	2. Strain through cheesecloth of triple thickness.
Cinnamon stick	1 1/2 inch	3. Store, covered, in refrigerator until needed.
Minced garlic	1 1/2 teaspoons	
Ginger root, broken in pieces	3 small	
Whole cloves	3	
Whole cardamom pods, split	3	
Ground turmeric	3/4 teaspoons	

Jamaica Barbecued Chicken

Yield: 48 portions

Featured Seasonings: lemon or lime juice, salt, ground allspice, garlic powder, onion powder, ground red pepper

Ingredients	Quantities	Procedure
Butter or margarine, melted	1 1/2 pounds	1. Combine all ingredients except chicken parts.
Lemon or lime juice	3/4 cup	
Salt	1/4 cup	
Ground allspice	2 tablespoons	
Garlic powder	2 tablespoons	
Onion powder	2 tablespoons	
Ground red pepper	1 1/2 teaspoons	
Chicken parts	30 pounds	2. Place chicken in shallow pans. Brush both sides with seasoned butter.
		3. Bake in a preheated 350°F. oven for 45 minutes, turning and brushing occasionally with seasoned butter.
		4. Serve garnished with sliced lemon, if desired.

Chicken Korma

Yield: 48 portions

Featured Seasonings: onions, garlic, curry powder, ground turmeric, ground black pepper, bay leaves, salt

Ingredients	Quantities	Procedure
Butter or margarine	1 1/2 cups	1. In a large skillet, heat butter and oil. Add chicken, a few pieces at a time; brown on all sides; remove and set aside.
Oil	1 1/2 cups	
Chicken parts	36 pounds	
Onions, chopped	2 quarts	2. Add onions and garlic along with curry powder, turmeric, black pepper, and bay leaves; cook and stir for 3 minutes.
Garlic, minced	2 tablespoons	
Curry powder	1 1/2 cups	
Ground turmeric	2 tablespoons	
Ground black pepper	1 1/2 teaspoons	
Bay leaves	12	
Plain yogurt	1 1/2 quarts	3. Remove from heat and stir in yogurt and salt.
Salt	1/4 cup	4. Add browned chicken pieces, spooning some of the sauce over the chicken. Simmer, covered, until chicken is fork-tender, about 35 minutes.
Steamed rice	As needed	5. Arrange chicken on a heated platter over steamed rice. Remove excess fat from sauce; spoon over chicken.

Adobo (Braised Chicken and Pork Casserole)

Yield: 48 to 60 portions

Featured Seasonings: shredded coconut, wine vinegar, soy sauce, salt, garlic, whole black peppercorns, bay leaves, ground black pepper

Ingredients	Quantities	Procedure
Shredded coconut	6 (3 1/2 oz.) cans	1. In a small sauce pot, combine coconut and water. Bring to the boiling point; reduce heat and simmer for 15 minutes. Pour through a strainer, pressing all the liquid from the coconut (makes about 2 1/4 quarts liquid); discard pulp.
Water	3 quarts	
Oil, salad	3/4 cup	2. In a large sauce pot, heat oil until hot. Add chicken, a few pieces at a time, browning well on all sides. Remove chicken; set aside.
Chicken parts	30 pounds	
Lean boneless pork shoulder, cut into 1-inch pieces	12 pounds	3. Add pork; brown well. Drain excess fat from sauce pot.
Wine vinegar	2 cups	4. Return chicken to sauce pot. Add reserved coconut liquid along with the vinegar, soy sauce, salt, garlic, peppercorns, bay leaves, and black pepper. Simmer, covered, until chicken and pork are tender, about 30 minutes. Serve with boiled rice, if desired.
Soy sauce	1 cup	
Salt	1/4 cup	
Garlic, minced	3 tablespoons	
Whole black peppercorns	36	
Bay leaves	12	
Ground black pepper	1 1/2 teaspoons	

Devilish Chicken Kiev with Green Peppercorns

Yield: 48 portions

Featured Seasonings: green peppercorns, butter, lemon juice, parsley, salt, ground black pepper

Ingredients	Quantities	Procedure
Green peppercorns, undrained	3 tablespoons	1. Crush peppercorns with spoon or in mortar with pestle.
Butter or margarine, softened	2 pounds	2. In a deep bowl, cream butter with peppercorns, 1/3 cup of the lemon juice, parsley, and 1 tablespoon of the salt; blend well. Divide mixture into 8 parts. Shape each part into a roll about 12 inches long. Wrap in plastic wrap or waxed paper; freeze until firm.
Lemon juice, divided	1 cup	
Parsley, finely chopped	1/2 cup	
Salt, divided	3 tablespoons	
Chicken breasts, split, boned, and skinned	24	3. Place each piece of chicken between paper; pound until thin. Sprinkle both sides of chicken with a blend of black pepper, remaining 2 tablespoons salt, and 2/3 cup lemon juice.
Ground black pepper	2 teaspoons	
		4. In the middle of each chicken breast, place a 2-inch piece of the butter mixture. Roll up and secure with toothpicks. Refrigerate until butter is firm.
Flour	As needed	5. Dredge each roll with flour, brush completely with egg, then roll in bread crumbs. Refrigerate until crumbs adhere, about 1 hour.
Eggs, beaten	6 to 8	
Fine dry bread crumbs	As needed	
Oil (for deep frying)	As needed	6. Heat sufficient oil for deep frying to 350°F. Fry chicken rolls a few at a time until chicken is golden brown, about 5 to 6 minutes.
		7. Serve immediately. (When knife is inserted into the cooked chicken, the butter should spurt out.)

Note: If desired, the stuffed and rolled breasts may be covered with freezer wrap and frozen. Before using, defrost, dredge with flour, brush with egg, and roll in bread crumbs as described in step 5; then proceed to chill and fry as directed.

Poulet Basilique (Chicken in Basil Wine Sauce)

Yield: 48 portions

Featured Seasonings: salt, ground white pepper, butter, dry white wine, basil leaves, onion powder

Ingredients	Quantities	Procedure
Chicken parts	35 pounds	1. Sprinkle chicken with salt and white pepper.
Salt	4 teaspoons	
Ground white pepper	2 teaspoons	
Butter or margarine, divided	3 pounds	2. In a large sauce pot, melt 2 pounds of the butter. Add chicken and brown slowly on all sides.
		3. Cover and cook slowly for another 25 to 30 minutes, stirring frequently to prevent butter from scorching.
		4. Remove chicken. Pour off any remaining butter in sauce pot.
Dry white wine	3 quarts	5. Add wine, basil, and onion powder to pot. Bring to the boiling point scraping pan juices into wine. Boil rapidly until wine is reduced to half. Swirl in remaining 1 pound butter. Season with additional salt and black pepper, if desired.
Basil leaves	1/2 cup	
Onion powder	4 teaspoons	
		6. Spoon sauce over chicken. Sprinkle with lemon juice, if desired.

Frosted Turkey Loaf

Yield: 48 portions

Featured Seasonings: aromatic bitters, onions, poultry seasoning, celery, pimiento, salt

Ingredients	Quantities	Procedure
Dry bread crumbs	2 gallons	1. Combine all ingredients except mashed potatoes; mix well.
Butter or margarine, melted	3 cups	2. Spoon mixture into 8 well-greased 9 x 5 x 2 1/2-inch loaf pans.
Milk or chicken broth	1 gallon plus 1 quart	3. Place pans into pans containing 1 inch of hot water. Bake in a preheated 350°F. oven until firm, about 45 minutes.
Aromatic bitters	3/4 cup	
Onions, minced	1 1/2 cups	4. Let loaves cool in pans for 10 minutes.
Poultry seasoning	3 tablespoons	
Celery, minced	1 quart	
Pimiento, chopped	1 quart	
Eggs, slightly beaten	3 dozen	
Cooked turkey, minced	1 1/2 gallons	
Salt	3 tablespoons	
Mashed potatoes, seasoned	2 gallons	5. Unmold loaves onto serving platters. With a spatula gently frost entire loaves with hot, seasoned mashed potatoes. (Frost sides of loaves first, then the tops.)
		6. Cut each loaf into 6 slices and serve hot with peas.

SEAFOOD

Zarzuela de Mariscos (Catalonian Seafood in Peppery Sauce)

Yield: 48 portions

Featured Seasonings: olive oil, onions, tomato sauce, brandy, garlic, salt, ground red pepper, anise seed

Ingredients	Quantities	Procedure
Fillet of sea bass, haddock, halibut, or sole	12 pounds	1. Cut fish into 2-inch pieces. Dredge in flour.
Flour	1 1/2 cups	
Olive oil, divided	2 1/4 cups	2. In a large skillet, heat 1 1/2 cups of the oil until hot.
		3. Add fish; cook until golden, about 10 minutes. Remove fish; set aside.
Raw shrimp, peeled and deveined	6 pounds	4. Add shrimp to skillet; cook until pink. Remove shrimp.
Onions, chopped	2 cups	5. Add remaining 3/4 cup oil to skillet. Stir in onions and garlic; sauté until tender.
Garlic, minced	3 tablespoons	
Tomato sauce	1 1/2 quarts	6. Stir in tomato sauce, water, brandy, salt, red pepper, and anise; bring to the boiling point. Stir in almonds, mussels, and clams. Simmer, covered, until shells open, about 5 to 6 minutes.
Water	1 quart	
Brandy	3/4 cup	
Salt	1 1/2 tablespoons	7. Return fish and shrimp to the skillet. Cover and cook until hot, about 3 minutes longer.
Ground red pepper	1 1/2 teaspoons	
Anise seed, crushed	1 teaspoon	8. Sprinkle with parsley and serve with rice, if desired.
Ground almonds or hazelnuts	1 1/8 cups	
Mussels	6 dozen	
Clams	6 dozen	

Fish Steaks in Curried Yogurt

Yield: 48 portions

Featured Seasonings: salt, onions, garlic, ground turmeric, cinnamon sticks, ground cardamom, ground black pepper, ground red pepper

Ingredients	Quantities	Procedure
Cod steaks	48 (6 to 8 oz. each)	1. Rub both sides of cod steaks with turmeric and 2 tablespoons of the salt.
Ground turmeric	1/4 cup	
Salt, divided	1/3 cup	
Oil, salad	3 cups	2. In a large skillet, heat oil until hot. Add cod steaks, a few at a time; brown about 3 minutes on each side. Remove and set aside.
Onions, chopped	2 quarts	3. In the same skillet in remaining oil, sauté onions and garlic until golden, about 3 minutes. Add yogurt, cinnamon, sugar, cardamom, black pepper, red pepper, and remaining salt. Cook and stir over low heat until hot, about 5 minutes.
Garlic, minced	1/2 cup	
Plain yogurt	1 gallon	
Cinnamon sticks (3-inch)	12	
Sugar	1/4 cup	4. Return cod to skillet. Spoon yogurt mixture over fish. Cover and simmer, until fish flakes easily when tested with a fork, about 6 minutes.
Ground cardamom	4 teaspoons	
Ground black pepper	1 tablespoon	
Ground red pepper	1 1/2 teaspoons	5. Serve over rice, if desired.

Seafood Teriyaki Ribbons

Yield: 48 portions

Featured Seasonings: teriyaki sauce, dry sauterne wine, lemon juice, parsley

Ingredients	Quantities	Procedure
Boneless white fish fillets, (sole, ocean perch, or cod)	12 pounds	1. Cut fish into strips, 1 to 2 inches wide. Allowing 4 ounces per serving, thread strips onto skewers in ribbon-like fashion.
Teriyaki sauce	2 cups	2. Combine teriyaki sauce, oil, wine, water, and lemon juice. Pour half of the mixture over the skewered fish; cover and refrigerate.
Salad oil	2 cups	
Dry sauterne wine	2 cups	
Water	1/2 cup	3. Broil fish, turning once and basting with marinade until it flakes easily with a fork.
Lemon juice	1/2 cup	
Cooked rice	As needed	4. Arrange fish on a bed of cooked rice and cap each skewer with a cherry tomato.
Cherry tomatoes	48	
Parsley, chopped	As needed	5. Heat remaining marinade to serve over fish and rice. Serve in separate sauce boat or spoon over. Sprinkle with chopped parsley.

Ch'ao-Yu-Pien (Chinese Fish Fillets)

Yield: 64 portions

Featured Seasonings: lemon juice, paprika, onion powder, anise seeds, salt, garlic powder, ground red pepper

Ingredients	Quantities	Procedure
Fish fillets	16 pounds	1. Cut fish into 2-inch pieces; dredge with flour.
Flour	3 cups	
Salad oil	3 cups	2. In a skillet, heat oil until hot. Add fish; fry until browned on both sides. Drain on paper toweling; set aside.
Water	1 gallon	3. Add remaining ingredients to skillet. Cover and simmer sauce for 20 minutes, stirring occasionally. (Add more water if necessary.)
Lemon juice	1 cup	
Paprika	1 cup	
Onion powder	2/3 cup	4. Add reserved fried fish. Heat only until hot.
Sugar	2/3 cup	5. Garnish with parsley, if desired.
Anise seeds, crushed	1/4 cup	
Salt	1/4 cup	
Garlic powder	4 teaspoons	
Ground red pepper	2 teaspoons	

Southern Fried Fish

Yield: 48 portions

Featured Seasonings: salt, ground black pepper, onion powder, parsley flakes, paprika

Ingredients	Quantities	Procedure
Flour	1 1/2 quarts	1. Mix flour with salt and black pepper.
Salt	2 tablespoons	
Ground black pepper	1 teaspoon	
Eggs, beaten	6	2. Combine eggs with evaporated milk.
Evaporated milk	1 quart	
Cracker meal	1 quart	3. Blend cracker and corn meals with onion powder, parsley, and paprika.
Yellow corn meal	2 cups	
Onion powder	1/3 cup	
Parsley flakes	1/2 cup	
Paprika	1/4 cup	
Fish fillets (turbot, flounder, or haddock	48 (4 to 6 ounces each)	4. Coat both sides of fish fillets with seasoned flour, then dip in egg and milk mixture, and then in corn meal mixture.
Fat for frying	As needed	5. Deep or shallow fry fish in fat heated to 365 °F. until golden brown.
		6. Serve sprinkled with chives, if desired.

Boston Cod Pie

Yield: 48 portions

Featured Seasonings: salt, bay leaves, celery, onions, butter, powdered mustard, vermouth, pimiento

Ingredients	Quantities	Procedure
North Atlantic cod or pollock fillets	8 pounds	1. Place frozen fish fillets with water, salt, and bay leaves in large covered skillets.
Water	2 quarts	
Salt	2 teaspoons	2. Bring water to the boiling point. Immediately reduce heat and simmer 6 to 8 minutes.
Bay leaves	8	
		3. Remove fish from liquid, drain, and flake.
Celery, minced	1 cup	4. Sauté celery and onions in butter. Stir in flour; cook and stir over low heat about 30 seconds. Add cream and powdered mustard. Continue cooking and stirring over low heat until mixture thickens.
Onions, minced	1 cup	
Butter or margarine	1 pound	
Flour	2 cups	
Light cream or milk	1 gallon	
Powdered mustard	2 teaspoons	
Walnuts, chopped	2 cups	5. Remove from heat and stir in nuts, vermouth, pimiento, and reserved flaked fish.
Vermouth	1/2 cup	
Pimiento, chopped	1/2 cup	
Pastry	8 pounds (for 2-crust, 8-inch pies)	6. Pour into pastry-lined 8-inch pie pans. Cover with top crusts; trim, then seal edges tightly, and flute. Cut steam vents in top of pie.
		7. Bake in preheated 400°F. oven 5 to 30 minutes.
		8. Allow pie to stand for 10 minutes before cutting.

Curried Peanut Fish

Yield: 48 portions

Featured Seasonings: salt, ground black pepper, curry powder

Ingredients	Quantities	Procedure
Natural (unbreaded) fish fillets	17 pounds	1. Thaw fish fillets, if frozen, and pat dry. Place in a baking pan.
Peanut butter	1 quart	2. Combine peanut butter, eggs, and milk until smooth. Add seasonings.
Eggs	10	
Milk	1 quart	
Salt	to taste	
Ground black pepper	to taste	
Curry powder	1/4 cup	
Peanuts, chopped	As needed	3. Spread over fillets, sprinkle with chopped peanuts.
		4. Bake in a preheated 375°F. oven until fish flakes easily when tested with fork, about 30 minutes.

Fillets a l'Orange

Yield: 50 portions

Featured Seasonings: orange juice, orange rind, lemon juice, salt, ground black pepper, ground nutmeg

Ingredients	Quantities	Procedure
Fish fillets	18 pounds (6 ounces each)	1. Place fish in greased baking pans.
Orange juice	1 quart	2. Combine and mix remaining ingredients; pour over fillets.
Orange rind, grated	1/2 cup	3. Bake in a preheated 350°F. oven until fish flakes easily when tested with fork, about 30 minutes.
Butter or margarine, melted	1 1/2 cups	
Lemon juice	2/3 cup	
Salt	3 tablespoons	
Ground black pepper	1 teaspoon	
Ground nutmeg	1/2 teaspoon	
Oranges, slices or wedges	To garnish	4. To serve, place a fillet on a plate; pour about 2 tablespoons sauce from pan over fish; garnish with orange slices or wedges.

Fillet of Sole, Bonne Femme

Yield: 48 portions

Featured Seasonings: salt, ground white pepper, dry white wine, onion, parsley flakes, garlic powder, butter, lemon juice

Ingredients	Quantities	Procedure
Fillet of sole	16 pounds	1. Sprinkle both sides of fish with salt and white pepper. Roll up fillets. Place in a buttered skillet.
Salt	3 tablespoons	
Ground white pepper	2 teaspoons	
Mushrooms, sliced	2 pounds	2. Add mushrooms, wine, minced onion, parsley flakes, and garlic powder. Bring to the boiling point. Reduce heat and simmer, covered, until fish flakes when tested with a fork, about 10 minutes.
Dry white wine	2 quarts	
Instant minced onion	1 cup	
Parsley flakes	1 cup	
Garlic powder	2 teaspoons	3. Remove fish and mushrooms to a steam table pan; keep warm.
		4. Reduce pan liquid to 2 quarts; set aside.
Butter or margarine	1 1/2 cups	5. In a sauce pan melt butter. Stir in flour; cook and stir for 2 minutes. Stir in reserved pan liquid and milk. Bring to the boiling point. Cook and stir until thickened.
Flour	2 cups	
Milk	1 1/2 quarts	
Egg yolks, lightly beaten	16	6. Remove from heat and stir in egg yolks, heavy cream, and lemon juice.
Heavy cream	1 quart	
Lemon juice	3 tablespoons	7. Pour sauce over fish and mushrooms. Place under a preheated hot broiler until sauce is lightly glazed, about 2 minutes.

Trout Amandine

Yield: 48 portions

Featured Seasonings: salt, ground black pepper, paprika, butter, lemon juice, parsley

Ingredients	Quantities	Procedure
Salt	3 tablespoons	1. Combine salt, black pepper, and paprika. Season trout with mixture.
Ground black pepper	1 teaspoon	
Paprika	2 teaspoons	
Ready-to-eat trout	48 (8 ounce)	
Flour	As needed	2. Roll trout in flour; shake off excess flour.
Oil	As needed	3. In a large skillet, pour in oil to depth of 1/4 inch. Add trout; sauté about 4 minutes on each side, turning once, adding more oil as needed.
Butter	2 pounds	4. To make sauce, melt butter. Add almonds; sauté lightly. Add remaining ingredients; mix well. Spoon over trout.
Almonds, sliced	3 cups	
Lemon juice	1/2 cup	
Parsley, chopped	1/2 cup	

Macaroni Salmon Bake

Yield: 48 portions

Featured Seasonings: onion, Worcestershire sauce, ground red pepper

Ingredients	Quantities	Procedure
Elbow macaroni	6 pounds	1. Cook macaroni until barely tender, following package directions; drain.
Condensed cheddar cheese soup	8 (11 oz.) cans	2. In a sauce pot, combine soup with milk; stir in onion, Worcestershire sauce, and red pepper. Heat, but do not boil.
Milk	2 1/4 quarts	
Instant minced onion	3/4 cup	
Worcestershire sauce	1/2 cup	
Ground red pepper	1/2 teaspoon	
Canned salmon, drained and chunked	6 (1 lb.) cans	3. In two 12x20-inch pans, combine drained macaroni with salmon and tomato. Pour soup mixture over all. Top with buttered bread crumbs.
Tomatoes, diced	2 1/2 pounds	
Buttered soft bread crumbs	3 cups	
		4. Bake, uncovered, in a preheated 375 °F. oven for 30 minutes.

Note: If desired, mixture may be baked in individual baking dishes.

Nasi Goreng

Yield: 48 portions

Featured Seasonings: salt, onion, curry powder, ground coriander, garlic, ground red pepper

Ingredients	Quantities	Procedure
Water	1 gallon and 1 quart	1. In a medium sauce pan, bring water to the boiling point; stir in rice and salt. Reduce heat and simmer, covered, until rice is tender, about 20 minutes.
Raw regular cooking rice	2 quarts	
Salt	3 tablespoons	
Salad or peanut oil	2 2/3 cups	2. Meanwhile, combine oil, minced onion, curry powder, coriander, minced garlic, and red pepper; mix well. Pour over chicken and shrimp; marinate while rice cooks.
Instant minced onion	1/2 cup	
Curry powder	1/2 cup	
Ground coriander	3 tablespoons	
Instant minced garlic	4 teaspoons	
Ground red pepper	1 teaspoon	
Cooked chicken, slivered	2 quarts	
Cooked shrimp, diced	2 quarts	
Eggs, lightly beaten	24	3. Make very thin omelets by pouring about 2 tablespoons egg into a lightly buttered small skillet. Fry until firm; repeat, using all of the eggs. Roll each omelet; cut into 1/4-inch wide slices; set aside.
Butter or margarine	As needed	
		4. In a large skillet, sauté chicken mixture for 3 minutes. Add rice; cook and stir until well blended and hot, about 3 minutes longer. Serve garnished with sliced omelets.

Poached Fish with Herbed Tomato Sauce

Yield: 48 portions

Featured Seasonings: vinegar, onions, celery, salt, fennel seed, parsley flakes, whole black pepper, ground thyme, bay leaves, Herbed Tomato Sauce

Ingredients	Quantities	Procedure
Water	3 gallons	1. In a large skillet, combine water with vinegar and seasonings. Bring to the boiling point.
Vinegar	3 cups	
Onions, minced	2 cups	
Celery, chopped	1/2 cup	
Salt	1/4 cup	
Fennel seed	3 tablespoons	
Parsley flakes	2 tablespoons	
Whole black pepper	2 tablespoons	
Ground thyme	2 teaspoons	
Bay leaves	2 large	
Fillet of flounder, sole, or fish steaks	14 pounds	2. Add fish. Reduce heat and simmer, covered, until fish flakes easily with a fork, about 10 minutes.
Herbed Tomato Sauce (see		
following recipe)	about 3 quarts	3. Remove fish to a steam table pan. Strain stock (court bouillon) and reserve for use in preparing Herbed Tomato Sauce (following recipe).

Herbed Tomato Sauce (for Poached Fish)

Yield: 48 portions

Featured Seasonings: parsley, bay leaves, salt, garlic powder, basil leaves, black pepper

Ingredients	Quantities	Procedure
Crushed canned tomatoes	3 quarts	1. Combine all ingredients in a sauce pot. Bring to the boiling point. Reduce heat and simmer, uncovered, until thickened, 25 to 30 minutes, stirring frequently. Remove bay leaves.
Court bouillon	1 quart	
Canned mushrooms	1 (1 lb.) can	
Parsley, chopped	1 cup	2. Serve hot over poached fish.
Bay leaves	2 large	
Salt	2 tablespoons	
Garlic powder	2 tablespoons	
Basil leaves	1 tablespoon	
Ground black pepper	1 teaspooon	

Indian Curried Shrimp

Yield: 36 to 48 portions

Featured Seasonings: onions, ground coriander seeds, ground cumin seeds, curry powder, ground red pepper, salt, ground cardamom

Ingredients	Quantities	Procedure
Shortening or salad oil	1 1/2 cups	1. In a large skillet, heat shortening until hot. Add onions; sauté until tender.
Onions, minced	1 quart	
Ground coriander seeds	3/4 cup	2. Stir in spices; sauté for 2 minutes longer. Remove skillet from heat. Add 1 1/2 quarts water; blend thoroughly. Cover and simmer for 20 minutes.
Ground cumin seeds	1/4 cup	
Ground cardamom	2 tablespoons	
Curry powder	2 tablespoons	
Ground red pepper	1 teaspoon	
Water	As directed	3. Add shrimp, salt, and an additional 3 cups water. Simmer until shrimp are just cooked.
Raw shrimp, peeled and deveined	12 pounds	
Salt	1/4 cup	
Evaporated milk	3 cups	4. Stir in evaporated milk just before removing from heat.
		5. Serve over hot cooked rice with chutney, if desired.

Quenelles de Poisson (French Fish Dumplings)

Yield: 96 dumplings

Featured Seasonings: butter, salt, ground nutmeg, ground white pepper, Sauce Nantua

Ingredients	Quantities	Procedure
Soft bread crumbs	3 1/2 quarts	1. In a sauce pot combine bread crumbs, milk, butter, salt, nutmeg, and white pepper. Cook and stir over low heat until mixture thickens, about 5 minutes. Pour into a large bowl; cover and chill.
Milk	1 1/2 quarts	
Butter or margarine	1 1/2 pounds	
Salt	3 tablespoons	
Ground nutmeg	1 tablespoon	
Ground white pepper	1 1/2 teaspoons	
Pike or halibut fillets	6 pounds	2. Meanwhile, push fish through the finest blade of a meat grinder. Mix fish with eggs.
Eggs, well beaten	18	
		3. Combine fish with bread mixture; cover and chill until firm.
		4. With wet hands shape fish mixture into 96 balls.
		5. In a large skillet bring 3 inches of water to a boil. Add fish balls, a few at a time. Simmer, uncovered, until they float to the top, about 10 minutes. Remove with a slotted spoon to a steam table.
Sauce Nantua (see following recipe)	1 gallon	6. Serve hot with Sauce Nantua. Garnish with whole shrimp, if desired.

Sauce Nantua (for Quenelles)

Yield: 1 gallon

Featured Seasonings: paprika, ground red pepper, parsley, salt

Ingredients	Quantities	Procedure
Butter or margarine	1 cup	1. In a medium sauce pot, melt butter. Add onions; sauté for 2 minutes. Add flour; cook and stir for 1 minute.
Onions, minced	1 cup	
Flour	1 cup	
Milk	2 quarts	2. Stir in milk. Cook and stir until mixture boils and thickens. Stir in cream, salt, paprika, and red pepper. Bring just to the boiling point; reduce heat and simmer, uncovered, for 3 minutes.
Heavy cream	1 quart	
Salt	1 tablespoon	
Paprika	1 tablespoon	
Ground red pepper	1/2 teaspoon	
Small shrimp, cooked and diced	1 quart	3. Stir in shrimp and parsley. Heat until hot. Serve over Quenelles.
Parsley, chopped	1 cup	

Really Fast Sole Chowder

Yield: 48 portions

Featured Seasonings: bay leaves, onions, salt

Ingredients	Quantities	Procedure
Frozen North Atlantic sole fillets	12 pounds	1. In a large sauce pot, place block of frozen sole fillets.
Water	1 gallon	2. Add water, mixed vegetables, onions, bay leaves, and salt. Cover and bring to a boil. Reduce heat immediately and simmer 6 to 8 minutes. With fork, gently break fish into bite-sized pieces.
Frozen mixed vegetables	3 (40 oz.) packages	
Onions, sliced	3 cups	
Bay leaves	8	
Salt	1 tablespoon	3. Stir in soup and sugar.
Canned condensed tomato soup	5 (50 oz.) cans	4. Cover and simmer until soup is heated thoroughly and vegetables are tender, 3 to 4 minutes.
Sugar	1 1/2 teaspoons	

Vischkoekjes (Dutch Fish Cakes)

Yield: 48 portions

Featured Seasonings: parsley, salt, ground black pepper, ground nutmeg

Ingredients	Quantities	Procedure
Fish fillets	8 pounds	1. Arrange fish in a single layer in large skillets.
Boiling court bouillon or water	As needed	2. Cover with court bouillon. Bring to the boiling point. Reduce heat and simmer, covered, until fish flakes, about 5 minutes. Remove fish from liquid. Flake with a fork.
Milk	1 quart	3. In a large bowl, pour milk over bread to soften. Add fish, eggs, butter, parsley, salt, black pepper, and nutmeg; mix well.
Sliced white bread	2 pounds	
Eggs, lightly beaten	16	
Butter or margarine, melted	1 cup	
Parsley, chopped	1 cup	
Salt	1/4 cup	
Ground black pepper	1 1/2 teaspoons	
Ground nutmeg	1 1/2 teaspoons	
Dry bread crumbs	As needed	4. Shape into 96 patties, using about 1/4 cup mixture for each fish cake. Coat generously with bread crumbs. Refrigerate at least 4 hours for crumbs to set.
Oil for frying	As needed	5. Fry fish cakes in hot oil 1/4-inch deep, until golden brown, about 2 or 3 minutes on each side. Drain.

Caldeirada (Portuguese Boatman's Stew)

Yield: 48 portions

Featured Seasonings: olive oil, onions, celery, green peppers, garlic, dry white wine, parsley, bay leaves, salt, crushed red pepper

Ingredients	Quantities	Procedure
Olive oil	2 cups	1. In a very large, heavy sauce pot, heat oil until hot. Add onions, celery, green peppers, and garlic; sauté until tender.
Onions, chopped	1 1/2 quarts	
Celery, chopped	1 1/2 cups	
Green peppers, chopped	1 1/2 cups	
Garlic, minced	1 1/2 tablespoons	
Water	2 gallons	2. Add water, wine, tomatoes, parsley, bay leaves, salt, and red pepper. Bring to the boiling point. Reduce heat and simmer, uncovered, for 20 minutes, stirring occasionally.
Dry white wine	3 cups	
Fresh tomatoes, peeled and diced	15 pounds	
Parsley, chopped	3/4 cup	
Bay leaves	12	
Salt	1/3 cup	
Crushed red pepper	1 1/2 teaspoons	
Potatoes, peeled and quartered	9 pounds	3. Add potatoes; cook 15 minutes longer.
Fillet of cod, halibut, or haddock, cut into 2-inch chunks	18 pounds	4. Add fish; cook another 15 minutes.
Cherrystone clams	72	5. Add clams and mussels; cook until potatoes and fish are done and clams and mussel shells are open, about 10 minutes.
Mussels	36	6. Serve with Portuguese flat bread, if desired.

Hot Dilled Shrimp in Shells

Yield: 48 portions

Featured Seasonings: onions, dry white wine, dill weed

Ingredients	Quantities	Procedure
Butter or margarine	1 1/2 cups	1. In a sauce pan, melt butter. Add onions and white wine; cook and stir until reduced by one third.
Onions, chopped	2/3 cup	
Dry white wine	2 quarts	
Medium white sauce	1 gallon	2. Add white sauce and dill.
Dill weed, chopped	2/3 cup	
Shrimp, cooked	12 pounds	3. Add shrimp; heat until hot, about 5 minutes.
Pastry shells, baked	48	4. Serve in individual pastry shells.

Jamaica Shrimp Stew

Yield: 48 portions

Featured Seasonings: onions, garlic, curry powder, parsley, salt, thyme leaves, ground red pepper, lemon juice

Ingredients	Quantities	Procedure
Butter or margarine	1 1/2 cups	1. In a large skillet, melt butter. Add onions, garlic, and curry powder; sauté for 5 minutes, stirring often.
Onions, chopped	1 quart	
Garlic, minced	2 tablespoons	
Curry powder	1 1/2 tablespoons	
Raw shrimp, peeled and deveined	12 pounds	2. Add shrimp, tomatoes, parsley, salt, thyme, red pepper, and lemon juice. Cover and simmer over moderate heat until shrimp turn pink, about 8 minutes, stirring occasionally.
Canned tomatoes, broken up	1/2 (No. 10) can	
Parsley, chopped	3/4 cup	3. Serve immediately over steamed rice, if desired.
Salt	1 tablespoon	
Thyme leaves	1 tablespoon	
Ground red pepper	1 teaspoon	
Lemon juice	1/3 cup	

SALADS & SALAD DRESSINGS

Herbed Vegetable Salad

Yield: 4 gallons

Featured Seasonings: red wine vinegar, lemon juice, salt, basil leaves, tarragon leaves

Ingredients	Quantities	Procedure
Carrots, sliced 1/2-inch thick	1 quart	1. In a large sauce pot of boiling, salted water, place carrots. Cook for 5 minutes. Add broccoli and cauliflower; cook for 2 minutes longer. Add zucchini; cook for 3 minutes longer. Drain vegetables and place in a bowl.
Broccoli flowerettes	1 quart	
Cauliflowerettes, sliced	1 quart	
Zucchini wedges, cut in 2-inch pieces	1 quart	
Oil, salad	1 cup	2. Combine oil, vinegar, lemon juice, salt, basil, and tarragon. Pour over vegetables. Cover and refrigerate until chilled, about 2 hours.
Red wine vinegar	1/2 cup	
Lemon juice	2 tablespoons	
Salt	2 1/2 teaspoons	3. Serve as an appetizer, salad, or with meat or poultry.
Basil leaves, crushed	2 1/2 teaspoons	
Tarragon leaves, crushed	1 teaspoon	

Greek Country Salad

Yield: 48 portions

Featured Seasonings: feta cheese, Greek salad dressing

Ingredients	Quantities	Procedure
Florida tomatoes	6 pounds	1. Use tomatoes held at room temperature until fully ripe. Remove stems; cut tomatoes into 1/2-inch thick slices. Cut each slice in half; set aside.
Head lettuce	6 pounds	2. Wash and drain lettuce. Break into bite-sized pieces; chill.
Leaf lettuce	3 pounds	
Cucumbers, sliced	6	3. At serving time, place greens in large individual salad bowls. Around the edge of the bowl, alternate tomato and cucumber slices. Place 4 pieces of feta cheese, 2 stuffed grape leaves, 1 halved lemon slice, a tomato half, and Greek olives over the top of the greens in any desired pattern. Toss with Greek Salad Dressing.
Feta cheese, cut in pieces	3 pounds	
Stuffed grape leaves	96	
Lemons, sliced	8	
Black Greek olives	2 pounds	
Greek Salad Dressing (see following recipe)	2 3/4 quarts	

Greek Salad Dressing

Yield: 2 3/4 quarts

Featured Seasonings: powdered mustard, wine vinegar, oregano leaves, salt, ground black pepper, garlic powder

Ingredients	Quantities	Procedure
Powdered mustard	2 tablespoons	1. Mix powdered mustard with an equal amount of warm water; let stand for 10 minutes for flavor to develop.
Salad oil	2 quarts	2. Combine mustard with remaining ingredients; mix well. Shake well before using.
Wine vinegar	3 cups	
Oregano leaves, crushed	1/4 cup	
Salt	4 teaspoons	
Ground black pepper	2 teaspoons	
Instant garlic powder	2 teaspoons	

Italian Dressing

Yield: 2 3/4 quarts

Featured Seasonings: wine or cider vinegar, powdered mustard, onion powder, salt, ground black pepper, garlic powder, Worcestershire sauce, lemon juice

Ingredients	Quantities	Procedure
Olive or salad oil	2 quarts	1. Combine all ingredients; blend well with a wire whip.
Wine or cider vinegar	3 cups	2. Shake or beat well just before serving.
Powdered mustard	2 tablespoons	
Onion powder	2 tablespoons	
Sugar	4 teaspoons	
Salt	4 teaspoons	
Ground black pepper	2 teaspoons	
Garlic powder	2 teaspoons	
Worcestershire sauce	1/3 cup	
Lemon juice	1 tablespoon	

Creamy Garlic Dressing

Yield: 3 quarts

Featured Seasonings: wine vinegar, lemon juice, onions, garlic cloves, prepared mustard, salt, ground black pepper

Ingredients	Quantities	Procedure
Wine vinegar	3 cups	1. In blender jar, combine vinegar, lemon juice, milk powder, onions, garlic, mustard, salt, sugar, and black pepper.
Lemon juice	1 cup	
Instant nonfat milk powder	1 cup	2. Blend until smooth, about 1 minute.
Onions, chopped	1 1/4 cups	
Garlic cloves, minced	8	
Prepared mustard	3 tablespoons	
Salt	2 tablespoons	
Sugar	4 teaspoons	
Ground black pepper	1 teaspoon	
Salad oil	5 1/2 cups	3. Blend in oil.

Creamy Salad Dressing

Yield: 1 3/4 quarts

Featured Seasonings: olive oil, tarragon vinegar, Dijon mustard, lemon juice, garlic powder, salt, powdered mustard, ground black pepper

Ingredients	Quantities	Procedure
Eggs	6	1. Place all ingredients except oil and heavy cream in electric blender container. Blend until smooth, about 30 seconds.
Olive oil	3/4 cup	
Tarragon vinegar	3/4 cup	
Dijon mustard	1/3 cup	
Lemon juice	3 tablespoons	
Garlic powder	2 tablespoons	
Sugar	1 1/2 tablespoons	
Salt	4 teaspoons	
Powdered mustard	3 teaspoons	
Ground black pepper	1/2 teaspoon	
Salad oil	2 1/4 cups	2. Gradually blend in oil and heavy cream; blend until smooth, about 30 seconds.
Heavy cream	3/4 cup	

Creamy French Dressing

Yield:	3 1/2 quarts
Featured Seasonings:	paprika, salt, garlic powder, ground white pepper, powdered mustard, cider vinegar, catsup, lemon juice, Worcestershire sauce

Ingredients	Quantities	Procedure
Eggs	8	1. In a large bowl, beat eggs with a wire whip until as thick as heavy cream.
Sugar	2 tablespoons	2. Add dry ingredients; beat until well-blended.
Paprika	2 tablespoons	
Salt	4 teaspoons	
Garlic powder	2 teaspoons	
Ground white pepper	2 teaspoons	
Powdered mustard	2 teaspoons	
Salad oil	2 quarts	3. Slowly stir in oil; beat until thick.
Cider vinegar	3 cups	4. Blend in vinegar, catsup, lemon juice, and Worcestershire sauce.
Catsup	1 cup	
Lemon juice	1/2 cup	5. Stir before serving.
Worcestershire sauce	1/2 cup	

Celery Slaw

Yield: 48 portions

Featured Seasonings: onions, powdered mustard, sour cream, lemon juice or vinegar (cider or wine), salt, ground white pepper

Ingredients	Quantities	Procedure
Celery, sliced	8 quarts	1. Combine celery, carrots, and onions in a large bowl.
Carrots, shredded	1 quart	
Onions, finely minced	1 cup	
Powdered mustard	3 tablespoons	2. Mix powdered mustard with warm water; let stand for 10 minutes for flavor to develop.
Warm water	3 tablespoons	
Mayonnaise or dairy sour cream	1 quart	3. Combine mustard with remaining ingredients; mix well. Pour over celery mixture. Toss gently.
Lemon juice or vinegar (cider or wine)	1 cup	
Sugar	1/2 cup	
Salt	2 tablespoons	
Ground white pepper	1 teaspoon	

Marinated Mushroom Salad

Yield: 4 quarts

Featured Seasonings: garlic, wine vinegar, oregano leaves, salt, ground black pepper

Ingredients	Quantities	Procedure
Instant minced garlic	3 tablespoons	1. Mix garlic with water; let stand for 10 minutes to rehydrate.
Water	3 tablespoons	
Fresh mushrooms or	6 pounds	2. Rinse, pat dry, and slice fresh mushrooms, or drain canned mushrooms; set aside.
Canned sliced mushrooms	5 (1 lb.) cans	
Olive or salad oil	3 cups	3. In a large sauce pot, heat oil. Add rehydrated garlic; sauté until lightly brown.
Wine vinegar	1 1/2 cups	4. Add mushrooms to hot oil; sauté for 2 minutes. Remove from heat. Add vinegar, oregano, salt, and black pepper; toss gently.
Oregano leaves	2 tablespoons	
Salt	2 tablespoons	
Ground black pepper	1 1/2 teaspoons	
Pimiento, diced	3/4 cup	5. Turn into bowl. Cover and marinate at least 2 hours. Remove from bowl and arrange on bed of fresh lettuce. Garnish with diced pimiento. Serve at room temperature.
Lettuce leaves	As needed	

Cardinal Salad

Yield: 48 portions

Featured Seasonings: salt, vinegar, celery, onions

Ingredients	Quantities	Procedure
Canned diced beets with juice	2 quarts	1. Drain beets, measuring juice. Add water to juice to make required amount of liquid.
Hot water and beet juice	3 1/2 quarts	
Orange gelatin	3 1/2 cups (1 1/2 pounds)	2. Dissolve gelatin and salt in hot liquid.
Salt	1 tablespoon	
Vinegar	1 cup	3. Add vinegar. Chill until slightly thickened.
Celery, diced	1 quart	4. Fold beets, celery, horseradish, and onions into gelatin.
Prepared horseradish	1/3 cup	5. Pour into individual molds or two 12x20x2 1/2-inch pans.
Onions, grated	1/3 cup	6. Chill until firm. Unmold, or cut in squares. Serve on lettuce with mayonnaise, if desired.

Sliced Avocados and Tomatoes
with Herbed French Dressing

Yield: 50 portions

Featured Seasonings: salt, oregano leaves, basil leaves, onion powder, garlic powder, ground black pepper, cider vinegar, lemon juice

Ingredients	Quantities	Procedure
Salt	4 teaspoons	1. Combine salt, oregano, basil, onion powder, sugar, garlic powder, black pepper, and oil. Let stand at least 1 hour for flavors to blend. Add vinegar and lemon juice. Mix well.
Oregano leaves, crumbled	2 tablespoons	
Basil leaves, crumbled	2 tablespoons	
Onion powder	2 tablespoons	
Sugar	4 teaspoons	
Garlic powder	2 teaspoons	
Ground black pepper	2 teaspoons	
Salad oil	2 quarts	
Cider vinegar	2 1/2 cups	
Lemon juice	1/2 cup	
Tomatoes, sliced	17 pounds	2. Arrange tomato and avocado slices on lettuce leaves. Spoon dressing over all.
Avocados, peeled and sliced	25	
Lettuce leaves	4 heads	

Taboulah Salad

Yield: 48 portions

Featured Seasonings: salad onions, lemon juice, honey, salt, mint flakes, ground cumin seeds, ground black pepper

Ingredients	Quantities	Procedure
Cracked wheat	2 cups	1. Soak cracked wheat in water for 1 hour or longer; drain if necessary.
Boiling water	2 quarts	
Salad onions, minced	1 cup	2. Rehydrate minced onions in water for 10 minutes.
Water	1 cup	
Olive or salad oil	2 1/2 cups	3. Add oil, lemon juice, honey, salt, mint, cumin, and black pepper; blend well.
Lemon juice	1 cup	
Honey	1/2 cup	
Salt	2 tablespoons	
Mint flakes, crumbled	2 tablespoons	
Ground cumin seeds	4 teaspoons	
Ground black pepper	2 teaspoons	
Lettuce, torn	2 gallons	4. In a salad bowl, combine lettuce, tomatoes, cucumbers and radishes.
Tomatoes, sliced	5 pounds	
Cucumbers, peeled and diced	3 cups	5. Sprinkle with cracked wheat.
Radishes, sliced	2 cups	6. Pour dressing over all. Toss gently and serve.

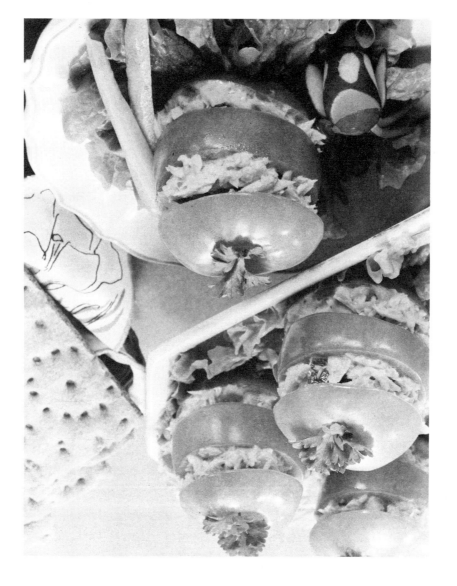

Triple Decker Tomato Salad

Yield: 48 portions

Featured Seasonings: celery, salt, ground black pepper

Ingredients	Quantities	Procedure
Medium-sized Florida tomatoes	48	1. Hold tomatoes at room temperature until fully ripe.
Canned tuna, drained and flaked	4 (15 oz.) cans	2. Combine remaining ingredients.
Hard-cooked eggs, chopped	1 1/2 quarts	3. Cut each tomato into 3 crosswise slices. Spoon tuna mixture on lower 2 slices. Reassemble tomatoes, covering with top slice.
Celery, finely chopped	1 quart	4. Serve on lettuce, if desired.
Mayonnaise	1 cup	
Salt	2 tablespoons	
Ground black pepper	1 teaspoon	

Herbed Spring Vegetable Chef's Salad

Yield:	48 portions
Featured Seasonings:	powdered mustard, wine vinegar, onion powder, crushed basil leaves, crushed marjoram leaves, garlic powder, salt, ground black pepper, Swiss cheese

Ingredients	Quantities	Procedure
Potatoes, peeled	12 pounds	1. Cook potatoes until tender; drain. Cut in large chunks. Place in a bowl.
Fresh asparagus or frozen asparagus	6 pounds 1 (40 oz.) package	2. Trim and cook fresh asparagus in boiling, salted water until crisp-tender, about 7 minutes; or cook frozen asparagus according to package directions. Drain and cut into 2-inch lengths; place in bowl with potatoes.
Powdered mustard	1 tablespoon	3. In a small bowl, combine mustard and warm water; let stand for 10 minutes to allow flavor to develop. Add oil, vinegar, onion powder, basil, marjoram, garlic powder, salt, sugar, and black pepper; mix well. Pour well-mixed dressing over vegetables; toss lightly. Cover and chill for 3 hours.
Warm water	1 tablespoon	
Oil, salad	2 cups	
Wine vinegar	1 cup	
Onion powder	1/4 cup	
Basil leaves, crushed	1/4 cup	
Marjoram leaves, crushed	2 tablespoons	
Garlic powder	2 tablespoons	
Salt	2 tablespoons	
Sugar	2 tablespoons	
Ground black pepper	1/2 teaspoon	
Cooked ham, thinly sliced	1 pound	4. Cut ham and cheese into strips; stir half into vegetable mixture.
Swiss cheese, thinly sliced	1 pound	
Lettuce leaves		5. Spoon vegetable mixture into individual lettuce-lined bowls. Garnish with remaining ham and cheese strips.

Hungarian Potato Salad

Yield: 48 portions

Featured Seasonings: powdered mustard, onions, sour cream, cider vinegar, paprika, salt, celery seeds, poppy seeds

Ingredients	Quantities	Procedure
Powdered mustard	4 teaspoons	1. Mix mustard with warm water; let stand 10 minutes for flavor to develop.
Warm water	4 teaspoons	
Onions, minced	3 cups	2. In a large bowl, combine potatoes, cucumbers, onions, and radishes; set aside.
Potatoes, cooked, peeled, diced	12 pounds (2 gallons)	
Cucumbers, peeled, diced	1 quart	
Radishes, diced	2 cups	
Hard-cooked eggs	1 cup	3. Separate egg yolks from whites. Dice egg whites and add to vegetable mixture.
Dairy sour cream	1 1/2 quarts	4. In a bowl, mash yolks. Stir in sour cream, vinegar, paprika, salt, and celery and poppy seeds; mix well. Add to vegetables; toss gently.
Cider vinegar	1/2 cup	
Paprika	1/3 cup	
Salt	1/4 cup	5. Cover and chill thoroughly. Serve on lettuce garnished with paprika, if desired.
Celery seeds	2 tablespoons	
Poppy seeds	2 tablespoons	

Marinated Bean Salad

Yield: 50 portions

Featured Seasonings: onion flakes, cider vinegar, marjoram leaves, ground black pepper

Ingredients	Quantities	Procedure
Red kidney beans	1 (No. 10) can	1. Drain kidney beans, reserving 5 cups of the liquid for later use.
Cooked frozen lima beans	1 (50 oz.) package	2. Combine kidney beans, lima beans, and green beans.
Cooked frozen cut green beans	1 (50 oz.) package	
Onion flakes	1 cup	3. Mix together reserved kidney bean liquid with remaining ingredients. Blend well. Pour over beans; toss lightly. Cover and refrigerate 12 hours.
Salad oil	2 cups	
Cider vinegar	2 cups	
Marjoram leaves, crumbled	1/2 cup	
Sugar	3 tablespoons	
Ground black pepper	2 tablespoons	

Dilled Cucumbers in Sour Cream

Yield: 48 portions

Featured Seasonings: salt, onion flakes, sour cream, white vinegar, dill weed, ground white pepper

Ingredients	Quantities	Procedure
Cucumbers	16 (about 12 pounds)	1. Peel and thinly slice cucumbers. Layer cucumbers in a bowl, sprinkling salt between each layer. Cover and refrigerate at least 2 hours.
Salt	3 tablespoons	
Onion flakes	1 cup	2. Rehydrate onion flakes in water for 10 minutes.
Water	1 cup	
Dairy sour cream	1 quart	3. Combine onion flakes with sour cream, vinegar, dill weed, sugar, and white pepper; blend well; set aside.
White vinegar	1 cup	
Dill weed	1/3 cup	4. Drain cucumbers. Add sour cream mixture, tossing to coat cucumbers.
Sugar	3 tablespoons	
Ground white pepper	1 teaspoon	5. Cover and refrigerate until well chilled, about 1 hour.

Abyssinian Lentil Salad

Yield: 48 portions

Featured Seasonings: salt, onions, red wine vinegar, ground black pepper, crushed red pepper

Ingredients	Quantities	Procedure
Water	5 quarts	1. In a medium sauce pan, bring water mixed with 4 teaspoons salt to a boil.
Salt, divided	1/4 cup	
Dried lentils	2 1/2 quarts	2. Add lentils. Reduce heat and simmer, covered, until lentils are firm but tender, about 25 minutes.
		3. Drain; rinse in cold water to cool; drain thoroughly.
Onions, chopped	1 cup	4. Combine onions, vinegar, oil, sugar, black pepper, red pepper, and remaining salt; blend well. Add lentils; toss. Cover and chill until ready to serve.
Red wine vinegar	2 cups	
Oil, olive	1 1/2 cups	
Sugar	3 tablespoons	5. Serve on lettuce-lined salad plates.
Ground black pepper	1 teaspoon	
Crushed red pepper	1/2 teaspoon	

Clam Stuffed Tomatoes

Yield: 48 portions

Featured Seasonings: salt, scallions, red hot pepper sauce

Ingredients	Quantities	Procedure
		1. Use tomatoes held at room temperature until fully ripe.
Medium-sized Florida tomatoes	48	2. Cut each tomato to resemble a flower by cutting into wedges almost through to the bottom; spread wedges slightly apart; sprinkle lightly with salt; set aside. In a bowl combine cottage cheese, clams, scallions, 2 teaspoons salt, and hot pepper sauce. Spoon into center of each tomato.
Salt	As needed	
Cottage cheese	8 pounds	
Canned minced clams, drained	8 (8 oz.) cans	
Scallions (green onions), sliced	2 cups	
Red hot pepper sauce	1/4 teaspoon	3. Serve on a bed of lettuce, garnished with parsley, if desired.

VEGETABLES

Cheddar Potatoes

Yield: 48 portions

Featured Seasonings: salt, cheddar cheese, freeze-dried chives, Worcestershire sauce

Ingredients	Quantities	Procedure
Dehydrated sliced potatoes	4 pounds	1. Scatter potatoes in large ovenproof pans. Sprinkle with salt, Pour water over potatoes; set aside.
Salt	2 teaspoons	
Boiling water	1 1/2 gallons	
Medium white sauce	1 gallon	2. Heat white sauce; stir in cheese, chives, and Worcestershire sauce. Pour over potatoes; mix well.
Cheddar cheese, grated	1 quart	
Freeze-dried chives	1/2 cup	3. Bake, uncovered, in a preheated 400°F. oven until potatoes are nicely browned and tender, 35 to 45 minutes.
Worcestershire sauce	1/2 cup	

African Spiced Raisin Rice

Yield: 48 portions

Featured Seasonings: onion, butter, cinnamon sticks, salt, lemon peel, ground turmeric

Ingredients	Quantities	Procedure
Instant minced onion	1 cup	1. Rehydrate onion in 1 cup water for 10 minutes.
Water	As directed	
Butter or margarine	2 cups	2. In a large skillet, melt butter. Add onion and rice; cook and stir only until pale gold.
Raw regular cooking rice	2 quarts	
Dark raisins	1 1/2 quarts	3. Stir in 4 1/2 quarts boiling water, raisins, cinnamon sticks, salt, lemon peel, and turmeric. Bring to the boiling point. Reduce heat and simmer, covered, until rice is tender, about 15 minutes. Stir in peanuts.
Cinnamon sticks (2-inch)	8	
Salt	2 tablespoons	
Lemon peel, grated	2 tablespoons	
Ground turmeric	2 teaspoons	4. Serve hot, garnished with sliced lemon, if desired.
Peanuts	1 quart	

Skillet Potatoes and Eggs

Yield: 48 portions

Featured Seasonings: salt, onion, paprika, ground black pepper

Ingredients	Quantities	Procedure
Medium-sized boiling potatoes, peeled and sliced 1/4-inch thick	16 pounds	1. In a large sauce pan, place potatoes in water to cover. Add half of the salt. Bring to the boiling point. Reduce heat and simmer, covered, until almost tender, about 20 minutes. Drain; cool potatoes slightly.
Water	As directed	
Salt, divided	3 tablespoons	
Instant minced onion	2 2/3 cups	2. Rehydrate minced onion in 2 2/3 cups water for 10 minutes.
Bacon slices	3 pounds	3. In a large skillet, fry bacon until crisp. Drain and crumble; set aside.
		4. Pour off all but 2 cups bacon drippings from skillet. Divide drippings between two large skillets; heat until hot.
Paprika	2 teaspoons	5. Add half of the potatoes, onion, and paprika to each skillet; fry until potatoes are golden, adding more drippings if needed.
Eggs	32	6. Combine eggs, black pepper, and remaining 1 1/2 tablespoons salt; beat until well blended. Pour over potatoes. Sprinkle reserved bacon over the top.
Ground black pepper	2 teaspoons	
		7. Cover and cook until eggs are set, about 5 to 6 minutes.

Yellow Rice

Yield: 48 portions

Featured Seasonings: salt, lemon peel, cinnamon sticks, ground turmeric, ground red pepper

Ingredients	Quantities	Procedure
Raw regular cooking rice	2 quarts	1. Stir rice into boiling water.
Boiling water	1 gallon plus 1 quart	
Salt	2 tablespoons	2. Add salt, lemon peel, cinnamon, turmeric and red pepper. Simmer, covered, until rice is tender, about 20 minutes.
Lemon peel, grated	2 tablespoons	
Cinnamon sticks (3-inch)	8	
Ground turmeric	1 tablespoon	
Ground red pepper	1/2 teaspoon	
Golden seedless raisins	1 1/2 quarts	3. Remove cinnamon sticks; stir in raisins, sugar, and butter.
Sugar	1 cup	
Butter or margarine	1 cup	

Pois et Riz (Guadeloupe Beans and Rice)

Yield: 48 portions

Featured Seasonings: onion, salt, garlic, thyme leaves, ground black pepper, bay leaves, whole red peppers

Ingredients	Quantities	Procedure
Dried red kidney beans	3 quarts	1. Rinse beans; drain well.
Water	2 1/4 gallons	2. In a sauce pot, combine beans, water, minced onion, salt, minced garlic, thyme, black pepper, bay leaves, and red pepper.
Instant minced onion	1 1/2 cups	
Salt	1/3 cup	3. Bring to the boiling point. Reduce heat and simmer, covered, until beans are almost tender, about 2 hours.
Instant minced garlic	2 tablespoons	
Thyme leaves, crumbled	1 tablespoon	
Ground black pepper	1 1/2 teaspoons	
Bay leaves	6	
Whole red peppers	6 (1 1/2-inch each)	
Raw regular cooking rice	1 1/2 quarts	4. Add rice. Simmer, covered, until rice is tender and all of the liquid is absorbed, about 20 minutes. (If necessary, add more water.)

Rice with Apples

Yield:	48 portions
Featured Seasonings:	butter, saffron, ground red pepper

Ingredients	Quantities	Procedure
Butter or margarine, divided	1 1/2 cups	1. In a large skillet, melt 1 cup of the butter. Add apples; sauté for 5 minutes, stirring constantly. Remove apples; set aside.
Apples, peeled, diced	1 gallon	
Raw regular cooking rice	2 quarts	2. In the same skillet, melt remaining 1/2 cup butter. Add rice; brown well, stirring constantly. Stir in broth, saffron, and red pepper. Bring to the boiling point. Reduce heat, simmer, covered, until rice is tender, about 20 minutes.
Hot chicken broth	5 quarts	
Saffron, crumbled	2 teaspoons	
Ground red pepper	1/2 teaspoon	3. Add reserved apples. Heat and serve.

Italian Green Beans and Potatoes

Featured Seasonings: onion, garlic, olive oil, basil leaves, salt, ground black pepper, Romano cheese

Ingredients	Quantities	Procedure
Onions, minced	1 quart	1. In a large sauce pot, heat oil until hot. Add onions and garlic; sauté for 2 minutes.
Garlic, minced	2 tablespoons	
Olive oil	3 cups	
Water	3 quarts	2. Stir in remaining ingredients except cheese. Bring to the boiling point. Reduce heat and simmer, covered, until potatoes and beans are tender, about 30 minutes.
Medium potatoes, peeled and quartered	12 pounds	
Green beans, trimmed	12 pounds	
Small tomatoes, diced	4 pounds	
Basil leaves, crumbled	1/2 cup	
Salt	5 tablespoons	
Ground black pepper	3 tablespoons	
Romano cheese, grated	3 cups	3. Stir in cheese.

Bean, Squash, and Corn Stew

Yield: 48 portions

Featured Seasonings: onions, garlic, basil leaves, oregano leaves, ground black pepper, salt

Ingredients	Quantities	Procedure
Dried navy or cranberry beans	3 quarts	1. In a sauce pot, combine beans with water. Bring to a boil. Reduce heat and simmer, covered, for 1 hour.
Water	3 1/2 gallons	
Olive or salad oil	2 cups	2. In a skillet, heat oil until hot. Add onions and garlic; sauté for 5 minutes. Stir in tomatoes, basil, oregano, and black pepper. Cook and stir until mixture thickens, about 10 minutes. Add to the beans along with the squash and salt.
Onions, chopped	2 quarts	
Garlic, minced	1/4 cup	
Canned tomatoes, broken up	1 (no. 10) can	
Basil leaves, crumbled	1 cup	3. Simmer, covered, until beans are tender, about 2 hours.
Oregano leaves, crumbled	1/4 cup	
Ground black pepper	2 teaspoons	
Winter squash, cut into 1-inch pieces	8 pounds	
Salt	1/4 cup	
Corn kernels	2 quarts	4. Add corn; cook 10 minutes longer.

Green Beans Atjar

Yield: 8 quarts

Featured Seasonings: salt, garlic, whole dried red pepper, curry powder, turmeric, fenugreek seeds, ground cumin, ground coriander

Ingredients	Quantities	Procedure
Fresh green beans	12 pounds	1. Trim ends from green beans. Place beans in large bowl; add boiling water to cover. Let stand for 2 minutes. Drain and rinse under cold water. Drain and return beans to bowl. Sprinkle with salt; stir well. Cover and let stand at room temperature for 2 hours.
Boiling water	As needed	
Salt	1/3 cup	
		2. Drain beans, pressing out excess water.
Instant minced garlic	1/4 cup	3. Rehydrate minced garlic in water for 10 minutes.
Water	1/4 cup	
Oil	2 1/2 quarts	4. In a sauce pot, heat oil just until a light haze forms on the surface. Add rehydrated garlic, red peppers, curry powder, turmeric, fenugreek, cumin, and coriander; sauté for 1 minute.
Whole dried red peppers (2-inch)	8	
Curry powder	3/4 cup	
Ground turmeric	1/4 cup	5. Add green beans; cook and stir until hot, about 5 minutes. Remove from heat, pack into jars or place in a large bowl.
Fenugreek seeds	2 tablespoons	
Ground cumin	4 teaspoons	6. Cover and refrigerate for at least 2 days before serving.
Ground coriander	2 teaspoons	

Polish Noodles and Cabbage

Yield:	48 to 64 portions
Featured Seasonings:	onion, butter, caraway seeds, salt, ground black pepper

Ingredients	Quantities	Procedure
Instant minced onion	2 cups	1. Rehydrate onion in water for 10 minutes.
Water	2 cups	
Cabbages	8 pounds	2. Meanwhile, shred cabbage (makes about 3 gallons).
Butter or margarine	1 pound	3. In a large skillet, melt butter. Add onion; sauté for 2 minutes. Add cabbage, caraway, salt, and black pepper; sauté until cabbage is tender, about 8 minutes, stirring occasionally.
Caraway seeds	3 tablespoons	
Salt	1 tablespoon	
Ground black pepper	1 teaspoon	
Medium-width egg noodles	4 pounds	4. Meanwhile, cook noodles in boiling, salted water following package directions; drain. Place in a large bowl. Add cabbage mixture; toss well.
		5. Serve with meat, poultry, or fish.

Mushrooms Rumanian Style

Yield: 48 portions

Featured Seasonings: fennel seeds, lemon juice, dry white wine, parsley, chives, onion powder, salt, ground black pepper

Ingredients	Quantities	Procedure
Olive or salad oil	2 cups	1. In a large skillet, heat oil until hot. Add mushrooms and fennel; sauté for 5 minutes.
Fresh mushrooms	8 pounds	
Fennel seeds, crushed	2 teaspoons	
Lemon juice	1 cup	2. Add lemon juice, wine, parsley, chives, onion powder, salt, and black pepper. Cook, stirring constantly, for 3 minutes.
Dry white wine	2 cups	
Parsley, chopped	1 cup	3. Serve with roast meats, if desired.
Chives, chopped	1/2 cup	
Onion powder	2 tablespoons	
Salt	2 teaspoons	
Ground black pepper	1/2 teaspoon	

Italian Cheese and Spinach Dumplings

Yield: 54 dumplings

Featured Seasonings: onion, garlic, ricotta cheese, parmesan cheese, parsley flakes, basil leaves, salt, ground nutmeg, ground black pepper

Ingredients	Quantities	Procedure
Instant minced onion	1/3 cup	1. Rehydrate minced onion and garlic in water for 10 minutes.
Instant minced garlic	3/4 teaspoon	
Water	1/3 cup	
Frozen chopped spinach	1 1/2 (3 lb.) packages	2. Cook spinach as package label directs; drain very thoroughly, pressing to squeeze out as much moisture as possible.
Ricotta cheese	3 pounds	3. Place spinach in a large bowl with rehydrated onion and garlic and remaining ingredients except flour; mix well. Cover and refrigerate until thoroughly chilled, at least 4 hours.
Soft bread crumbs	1 1/2 quarts	
Eggs, lightly beaten	9	
Parmesan cheese, grated	1 cup	
Parsley flakes	1/2 cup	
Basil leaves, crumbled	2 tablespoons	
Salt	1 tablespoon	
Ground nutmeg	3/4 tcaspoon	
Ground black pepper	1/2 teaspoon	
All-purpose flour	1 1/2 cups	4. Shape into 3x1-inch lengths (makes about 18). Roll in flour.
		5. Drop into boiling, salted water to form one layer. After they float to the surface, cook for 5 minutes.
		6. Using a slotted spoon, lift out the cooked dumplings, letting them drain well. Place in an ovenproof casserole. Cover and keep warm in a slow oven until all dumplings are cooked.
		7. Serve with melted butter and grated Parmesan cheese, if desired.

Locro de Choclo (South American Succotash)

Yield: 48 portions

Featured Seasonings: onion, sweet pepper flakes, garlic, olive oil, salt, oregano leaves, paprika, cumin seeds, ground black pepper

Ingredients	Quantities	Procedure
Instant minced onion	1 cup	1. Rehydrate minced onion, pepper flakes, and garlic in water for 10 minutes.
Sweet pepper flakes	1 cup	
Instant minced garlic	2 tablespoons	
Water	2 cups	
Olive oil	1 1/2 cups	2. In a sauce pot heat oil until hot. Add rehydrated vegetables; sauté for 5 minutes.
Canned tomatoes, broken up	1 (no. 10) can	3. Stir in tomatoes, pumpkin, sugar, salt, oregano, paprika, cumin, and black pepper. Bring to the boiling point. Reduce heat and simmer, covered, until pumpkin is tender, about 15 minutes.
Pumpkin or winter squash, peeled and cubed	2 quarts	
Sugar	2 tablespoons	
Salt	2 tablespoons	
Oregano leaves, crumbled	2 tablespoons	
Paprika	2 tablespoons	
Cumin seeds, crushed	2 teaspoons	
Ground black pepper	2 teaspoons	
Canned or frozen corn kernels	1 1/2 gallons	4. Stir in corn and lima beans. Return to the boiling point. Reduce heat and simmer, covered, 5 minutes longer.
Frozen baby lima beans, thawed	1 (40 oz.) package	

Carciofi al Tegame alla Romana
(Baked Stuffed Artichokes)

Yield: 48 portions

Featured Seasonings: salt, lemon juice, onion, garlic, parsley flakes, mint flakes, ground black pepper

Ingredients	Quantities	Procedure
Medium-sized artichokes	48	1. Cut stems from artichokes so they stand upright. Cut off about 1 inch from across tops. Peel off any loose outer leaves. With scissors, trim about 1/4 inch from the tips of the leaves.
Water	As directed	2. In a large kettle of boiling water, add about 1/4 cup each of salt, oil, and lemon juice. Add artichokes. Cover and parboil, about 15 minutes. Remove artichokes from water, and let drain upside down until cool enough to handle.
Salt	As directed	
Oil	As directed	
Lemon juice	As directed	
Instant minced onion	2 1/4 cups	3. Meanwhile, make filling as follows: Rehydrate minced onion and garlic in 2 1/2 cups water for 10 minutes. In a large skillet, heat 2 cups oil; add rehydrated onion and garlic; sauté for 3 minutes. Add veal; brown, stirring constantly, about 3 minutes. Stir in 3 gallons water, peas, parsley, mint, black pepper, and 1/3 cup salt. Cook and stir for 5 minutes. Remove from heat; set aside.
Instant minced garlic	2 tablespoons	
Ground veal	6 pounds	
Frozen peas, thawed	12 (10 oz.) packages	
Parsley flakes	1 1/2 cups	
Mint flakes	1/4 cup	
Ground black pepper	1 tablespoon	

4. Gently spread the top leaves of the artichoke apart and pull out the thistlelike portion. With a spoon, scoop out the furry chokes. Fill center and some of the outside leaves with the veal mixture. Stand stuffed artichokes in a shallow baking pan with enough boiling water to come 1 inch up the sides of the artichokes. Cover with foil.

5. Bake in a preheated 350°F. oven until artichokes are tender, about 1 hour.

6. Serve hot with lemon wedges.

Baked Eggplant, Tomato, and Chick Pea Casserole

Yield: 48 portions

Featured Seasonings: onion powder, salt, garlic powder, ground black pepper, sesame seeds

Ingredients	Quantities	Procedure
Olive or salad oil	2 quarts	1. In a large skillet, heat oil. Add eggplant; cook until lightly browned on all sides, about 5 minutes. Remove to 20x12x2-inch baking pan.
Eggplants, cut into 2-inch pieces	16 pounds	
Onion powder	1 cup	2. Combine onion powder, salt, garlic powder, and black pepper. Sprinkle half over eggplant.
Salt	1/2 cup	
Garlic powder	4 teaspoons	
Ground black pepper	2 teaspoons	
Canned chick peas, drained	1 (no. 10) can	3. Scatter chick peas over the eggplant. Pour tomatoes over all. Sprinkle with remaining onion mixture. Top with sesame seed.
Canned tomatoes, broken up	1 (no. 10) can	
Sesame seeds	1 cup	4. Bake, uncovered, in a preheated 400°F. oven until eggplant is tender, about 50 minutes.

DESSERTS

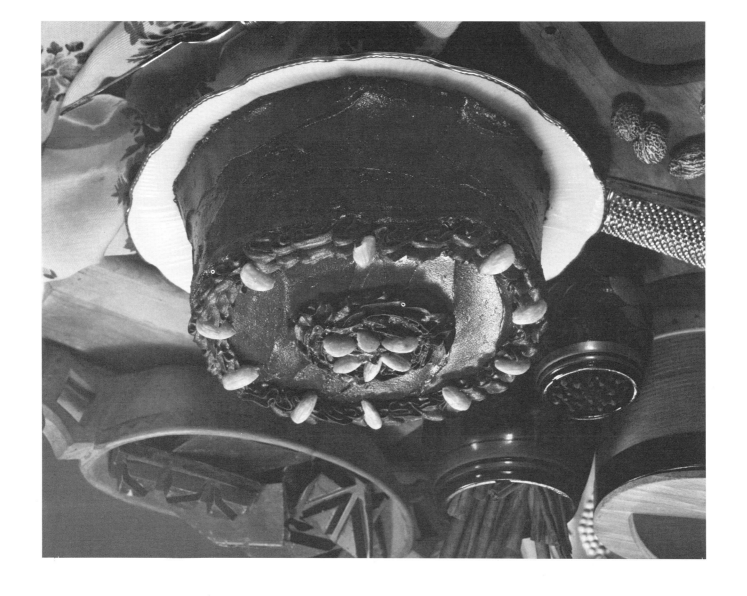

Shokolado Mindalny Tort
(Russian Spiced Chocolate Almond Cake)

Yield: six 8-inch cakes

Featured Seasonings: unsweetened chocolate, pure vanilla extract, ground cinnamon, ground nutmeg, ground cloves

Ingredients	Quantities	Procedure
		1. Generously grease and flour six 8-inch spring-form pans; set aside.
Butter or margarine, softened	1 1/2 pounds	2. In a large bowl, cream butter and sugar until fluffy. Beat in egg yolks; mix well. Mix in potatoes, almonds, chocolate, milk, and vanilla extract.
Sugar	2 quarts	
Eggs, separated	24	
Mashed potatoes, unseasoned, at room temperature	1 1/2 quarts	
Ground almonds	1 1/2 quarts	
Unsweetened chocolate, melted and cooled	1 1/2 pounds	
Milk	3 cups	
Pure vanilla extract	2 tablespoons	
Cake flour	2 1/4 quarts	3. Combine flour, baking powder, cinnamon, nutmeg, and cloves. Add to chocolate mixture; mix well.
Baking powder	1/4 cup	
Ground cinnamon	2 tablespoons	4. In a bowl, beat egg whites until stiff but not dry. Fold into batter.
Ground nutmeg	1 1/2 teaspoons	
Ground cloves	1 teaspoon	5. Pour into prepared pans; smooth with a spatula.
		6. Bake in a preheated 325 °F. oven until a cake tester inserted into center comes out clean, about 1 hour and 15 minutes.
		7. Place on a rack; let stand for 10 minutes. Remove sides of pans and let cool to room temperature.
Apricot preserves or orange marmalade, melted	3 cups	8. With a serrated knife, cut each cake into 2 layers. Spread one layer with preserves; top with second layer. Spread the sides and tops with Cinnamon Mocha Frosting. Garnish with blanched almond halves, if desired.
Cinnamon mocha frosting (see following recipe)		

Cinnamon Mocha Frosting

Ingredients	Quantities	Procedure
Butter or margarine, softened	1 pound and 2 ounces	1. In a small bowl, cream butter and sugar. Beat in coffee, chocolate, cinnamon, and vanilla extract.
Confectioners' sugar	3 1/2 quarts	
Strong coffee, cooled	1 1/2 cups	2. Refrigerate until firm enough to spread easily, about 15 minutes.
Unsweetened chocolate, melted and cooled	12 ounces	
Ground cinnamon	1 tablespoon	
Pure vanilla extract	2 tablespoons	

Mjuk p Pparkaka (Swedish Spice Cake)

Yield: four 9 1/2-inch cakes

Featured Seasonings: pure vanilla extract, salt, ground cinnamon, ground cardamom, ground ginger, ground cloves, sour cream

Ingredients	Quantities	Procedure
Fine dry bread crumbs	As needed	1. Generously butter four 9 1/2-inch bundt pans or four 10-inch tube pans; sprinkle with bread crumbs; shake out excess; set pans aside.
Butter or margarine, softened	1 1/2 pounds	2. In a mixing bowl, cream butter and sugar until light and fluffy. Add eggs gradually, beating well after each addition. Stir in vanilla extract.
Sugar	1 1/2 quarts	
Eggs	20	
Pure vanilla extract	1/4 cup	
All-purpose flour	2 1/2 quarts	3. Sift flour with baking soda, salt, and spices. Add to sugar mixture alternately with sour cream, beginning and ending with flour.
Baking soda	2 tablespoons	
Salt	4 teaspoons	
Ground cinnamon	1/3 cup	4. Spoon batter into prepared pans.
Ground cardamom	3 tablespoons	5. Bake in a preheated 325 °F. oven until a cake tester inserted into the center comes out clean, about 1 hour.
Ground ginger	2 tablespoons	
Ground cloves	1 tablespoon	6. Cool in pans for 10 minutes. Remove cakes from pans to racks; cool completely.
Dairy sour cream	1 1/2 quarts	
		7. Dust tops of cakes lightly with confectioners sugar, if desired.

Swedish Coffee Cake

Yield: six 9-inch coffee cakes

Featured Seasonings: ground cardamom seeds, butter

Ingredients	Quantities	Procedure
		1. Butter and lightly flour six 9-inch square cake pans; set aside.
Unsifted all-purpose flour	3 quarts	2. Sift flour, baking powder, and cardamom; set aside.
Baking powder	2 tablespoons	
Ground cardamom seeds	2 tablespoons	
Butter or margarine, softened	3 pounds	3. In a large mixing bowl, cream butter; gradually add 6 cups of the sugar, beating until light and fluffy. Beat in egg yolks. Add flour mixture in thirds; beat at low speed for 1 minute after each addition.
Sugar, divided	8 cups	
Eggs, separated	18	
		4. Beat egg whites until stiff but not dry; gently fold into flour mixture.
Chopped blanched almonds	1 1/2 cups	5. Spread batter into prepared pans. Sprinkle tops with remaining 2 cups sugar mixed with almonds.
		6. Bake in a preheated 350°F. oven until a cake tester inserted in center comes out clean, about 40 minutes.
		7. Cool in pans for 10 minutes. Turn out onto wire racks to cool. Serve warm.

Rich Greek Butter Cookies

Yield: 18 dozen

Featured Seasonings: unsalted butter, brandy, whole cloves

Ingredients	Quantities	Procedure
Unsalted butter or margarine, softened	2 pounds	1. In a mixing bowl, cream butter with sugar until light and fluffy (mixture should resemble whipped cream). Blend in egg yolks, brandy, and baking powder; mix well. Add almonds. Gradually add flour; continue blending in mixer if possible, or work in remaining flour with hands or pastry blender.
Confectioners sugar	1 cup	
Egg yolks	4	
Brandy	1/4 cup	
Baking powder	4 teaspoons	
Almonds, finely ground	2 cups	2. Turn dough onto a lightly floured board; knead until firm, about 10 minutes.
All-purpose flour, sifted	2 1/2 quarts	
Whole cloves	As needed	3. Shape dough into walnut-sized balls; stud each ball with a whole clove.
		4. Place on ungreased cookie sheets.
		5. Bake in a preheated 350°F. oven until browned, about 20 minutes.
Confectioners sugar	As needed	6. Cool slightly. Dust overall in confectioners sugar.

Note: If desired, add 2 teaspoons ground cloves to butter mixture in place of the whole cloves.

Almbuttertorte (Austrian Chocolate Cake)

Yield: four 9-inch cakes

Featured Seasonings: unsweetened cocoa, salt, ground cinnamon, ground nutmeg, pure vanilla extract, prepared butter cream

Ingredients	Quantities	Procedure
		1. Line bottoms of four 9-inch spring-form pans with lightly greased waxed paper; set aside.
Cake flour	2 cups	2. Sift flour with cocoa, cornstarch, baking powder, salt, and spices; set aside.
Unsweetened cocoa	1 cup	
Cornstarch	1/4 cup	
Baking powder	4 teaspoons	
Salt	1 teaspoon	
Ground cinnamon	1 tablespoon	
Ground nutmeg	1/2 teaspoon	
Eggs, separated	16	3. In a large mixing bowl, beat egg whites until soft peaks form. Gradually add half of the sugar; beat until stiff; set aside.
Sugar, divided	3 cups	4. In a small bowl, beat egg yolks and vanilla extract until thick and lemon-colored. Gradually add remaining sugar; beat well. Slowly pour in water while beating; beat for 1 minute. Gently fold into egg whites.
Pure vanilla extract	2 tablespoons	
Water	1/2 cup	
Apricot jam	1 1/3 cups	
Prepared butter cream	2 to 3 quarts	
		5. Add flour mixture in thirds, gently folding after each addition.
		6. Turn batter into four prepared pans.
		7. Bake in a preheated 350°F. oven until done, 30 to 40 minutes.

Spice Cookies

Yield: 96 cookies

Featured Seasonings: pure vanilla extract, ground cinnamon, ground nutmeg, ground cloves, salt

Ingredients	Quantities	Procedure
Eggs	6	1. In a large mixing bowl, beat eggs until light; gradually beat in sugar until mixture is pale and thick. Stir in vanilla extract.
Sugar	3 cups	
Pure vanilla extract	1 tablespoon	
All-purpose flour	6 cups	2. Mix flour with spices, baking powder, and salt. Add to egg mixture, blending well. (Dough should be smooth, but not sticky.) Chill for 1 hour.
Ground cinnamon	1 tablespoon	
Ground nutmeg	1/2 teaspoon	
Ground cloves	1/4 teaspoon	
Baking powder	1 1/2 teaspoons	
Salt	1/2 teaspoon	
Confectioners sugar		3. Sprinkle pastry board with confectioners sugar. Roll dough 1/2 inch thick. Make design with springerle roller; cut into squares where marked or cut into diamonds with sharp knife. Place cookies on greased baking sheets.
		4. Bake in a preheated 325 °F. oven until edges are golden, 15 to 20 minutes.
		5. Cool on wire racks. Store in airtight container. (Cookies may be stored for several months.)

Hungarian Poppy Seed Tea Roll

Yield:	six 16-inch rolls
Featured Seasonings:	poppy seed filling

Ingredients	Quantities	Procedure
Milk	1 1/2 cups	1. Scald milk; cool to lukewarm.
Active dry yeast	6 packages	2. Sprinkle yeast over water. Add 2 tablespoons sugar; stir until dissolved; let stand for 5 minutes.
Warm water	1 1/2 cups	
Sugar	2 tablespoons	
All-purpose flour	3 7/8 quarts	3. Sift flour with 1 cup sugar and salt. Cut in butter until mixture resembles coarse meal.
Sugar	1 cup	
Salt	1 1/2 teaspoons	
Butter or margarine	1 pound	
Eggs, slightly beaten	6	4. Add lukewarm milk and eggs to the yeast mixture. Gradually add the yeast mixture to the flour mixture; blend well.
		5. On a lightly floured board, knead dough until smooth. Place in a greased bowl. Turn dough so that greased side is up. Cover and let rise in a warm place until doubled in bulk.
Canned poppy seed filling	1 1/2 quarts	6. Punch dough down. Divide dough into 6 portions. On a lightly floured board, roll each portion into a 10x16-inch rectangle. Spread with Poppy Seed Filling. Roll, jelly roll fashion; seal ends.
		7. Bake in a preheated 350°F. oven until done, 30 to 40 minutes.

English Gingered Brandy Snaps

Yield: about 90 cookies

Featured Seasonings: unsulphured molasses, ground ginger, ground nutmeg, brandy

Ingredients	Quantities	Procedure
Butter or margarine	1 1/2 cups	1. In a medium sauce pan, combine butter, sugar, corn syrup, and molasses. Heat over medium heat just until butter melts.
Sugar	1 1/2 cups	
Light corn syrup	3/4 cup	
Unsulphured molasses	2 tablespoons	
All-purpose flour	3 cups	2. In a bowl combine flour, ginger, and nutmeg; stir into butter mixture. Blend in brandy.
Ground ginger	1 tablespoon	
Ground nutmeg	3/4 teaspoon	3. Drop by teaspoonfuls, 6 inches apart, onto greased cookie sheets.
Brandy	1/3 cup	
		4. Bake in a preheated 350°F. oven until golden, 8 to 10 minutes.
		5. Let cool for about 30 seconds.
		6. Ease cookies off pan with a spatula; then immediately roll loosely around the greased handle of a wooden spoon with the upper surface of each brandy snap on the outside.
		7. Cool on wire racks.
Whipped cream	3 quarts	8. Pipe whipped cream into cavity from each end using a pastry bag fitted with a star tube.
Sugar	1/3 cup	

Note: If brandy snaps begin to harden before they are rolled, return to oven for 30 seconds to soften again.

Grasshopper Pie

Yield: twelve 9-inch pies

Featured Seasonings: salt, pure vanilla extract, white creme de cacao liqueur, green creme de menthe liqueur

Ingredients	Quantities	Procedure
Lemon gelatin	3 1/2 cups	1. Dissolve gelatins, sugar, and salt in hot water. Cool.
Lime gelatin	3 1/2 cups	
Sugar	1 cup	
Salt	1 teaspoon	
Hot water	1 1/2 gallons	
Pure vanilla extract	2 tablespoons	2. Add vanilla and liqueurs. Chill until slightly thickened.
White creme de cacao liqueur	2 cups	
Green creme de menthe liqueur	2 cups	
Whipped topping mix	1 (8.4 oz.) bag	3. Prepare whipped topping mix as directed on bag. Blend in gelatin mixture.
Baked 9-inch pie shells, cooled	12	4. Ladle into pie shells, allowing about 1 quart per pie.
		5. Chill until firm. Garnish with additional prepared whipped topping, if desired.

Melopitta (Greek Apple Pie)

Yield: 48 portions

Featured Seasonings: salt, ground cinnamon, ground nutmeg, ground anise, honey

Ingredients	Quantities	Procedure
All-purpose flour	1 gallon	1. In a medium bowl, mix flour and 1 teaspoon of the salt. Cut butter into flour until mixture resembles coarse cornmeal. Gradually add 1 cup water; stir until mixture clings together and forms a smooth ball. If dough feels soft, wrap in plastic wrap and refrigerate until firm, about 15 minutes.
Salt, divided	3 teaspoons	
Butter or margarine	3 pounds	
Cold water	As needed	
		2. Roll out 2/3 of the dough to make a 16x24-inch rectangle. Ease into a 12x20-inch pan. Roll out remaining dough into a 14x22-inch rectangle; set aside.
Baking apples, sliced	3 1/2 gallons	3. In a bowl, combine apple slices, brown sugar, cinnamon, nutmeg, anise, and remaining 2 teaspoons salt.
Firmly packed brown sugar	2 quarts	
Ground cinnamon	1/4 cup	4. Top with remaining dough. Spoon into dough-lined baking pan. Crimp edges to seal. Cut an apple or other design on the top or cut several slits for steam to escape.
Ground nutmeg	4 teaspoons	
Ground anise	2 teaspoons	
Eggs	2	5. Beat eggs with 1 tablespoon water; brush over top.
		6. Bake in a preheated 400 °F. oven until top is golden, about 45 minutes. Cool on a rack until warm.
Honey	1 quart	7. Cut warm pie into rectangles. Serve with warm honey and yogurt.
Plain yogurt	64 ounces	

Layered Chocolate-Almond Liqueur Pie

Yield: six 9-inch pies

Featured Seasonings: salt, creme de cacao liqueur, semi-sweet chocolate mini-chips, almond liqueur

Ingredients	Quantities	Procedure
Plain gelatin	6 tablespoons	1. Soften gelatin in 3 cups of the milk.
Milk, divided	3 quarts	
Eggs, separated	18	2. In a sauce pan, combine egg yolks with sugar, salt, and remaining milk. Beat until well mixed. Cook over low heat, stirring constantly, until thickened.
Sugar	2 cups	
Salt	3/4 teaspoon	
		3. Add softened gelatin; stir until dissolved. Chill until custard begins to set.
Heavy cream	3 cups	4. Beat egg whites until stiff. Whip cream; fold whites and cream into custard.
Creme de cacao liqueur	1 1/2 cups	5. Divide custard into 2 equal portions. Into one part, mix the creme de cacao; spoon into pie shells. Sprinkle with semi-sweet chocolate.
Baked 9-inch pie shells	6	
Semi-sweet chocolate mini-chips	1 cup	
Almond liqueur	1 1/2 cups	6. Into the remaining custard, mix the almond liqueur; spoon over the first layer. Sprinkle with toasted slivered almonds. Chill several hours until firm.
Toasted slivered almonds	1 cup	

Macaroon Stuffed Peaches

Yield: 48 portions

Featured Seasonings: coconut macaroon crumbs, ground cinnamon, ground nutmeg, dry white wine, cinnamon sticks

Ingredients	Quantities	Procedure
Canned cling peach halves	2 (No. 10) cans	1. Drain peaches, reserving 6 cups of the syrup; set aside.
Coconut macaroon crumbs	1 1/2 quarts	2. In a bowl, combine macaroon crumbs, candied fruit, cinnamon, and nutmeg; mix well.
Mixed candied fruit, finely chopped	1/2 cup	
Ground cinnamon	1 tablespoon	3. Spoon stuffing into half of the peaches. Top with remaining peach halves. Arrange in a baking pan; set aside.
Ground nutmeg	1 1/2 teaspoons	
Dry white wine	3 cups	4. In a sauce pan, combine reserved syrup with wine and cinnamon sticks; bring to the boiling point. Reduce heat and simmer for 5 minutes.
Cinnamon sticks (2-inch)	6	
		5. Pour syrup over peaches. Bake, uncovered, in a preheated 350 °F. oven 20 to 25 minutes, basting occasionally.
		6. Serve warm or cold.

Sweet Potato Squares

Yield: 48 portions

Featured Seasonings: butter, salt, ground cinnamon, ground ginger, anise seeds, ground cloves, coconut milk

Ingredients	Quantities	Procedure
Sweet potatoes, solid pack	1 (No. 10) can	1. In a large mixing bowl, combine sweet potatoes and pumpkin. Pour in butter; mix well. Add eggs, beating well.
Mashed pumpkin	1 (No. 10) can	
Butter or margarine, melted	1 1/2 cups	
Eggs, beaten	12	
Sugar	1 3/4 quarts	2. Combine sugar, flour, salt, and spices; stir into the mixture. Add coconut milk; mix well.
Flour	1 cup	
Salt	2 tablespoons	3. Turn into buttered casseroles.
Ground cinnamon	1 tablespoon	4. Cover and bake in a preheated 400°F. oven for 1 3/4 hours.
Ground ginger	1 tablespoon	5. Cool completely. Slice and serve as dessert, with whipped cream if desired.
Anise seeds, crushed	1 teaspoon	
Ground cloves	1 teaspoon	
Coconut milk* or light cream	1 quart	

*To make coconut milk; pour 2 quarts hot water over 3 quarts grated fresh coconut or 2 quarts flaked or shredded coconut. Let stand until cold. Turn into a large cheesecloth square and squeeze out milk.

Amber Pie

Yield: six 9-inch pies

Featured Seasonings: ground cinnamon, ground cloves, ground nutmeg, lemon juice

Ingredients	Quantities	Procedure
Sugar, divided	3 cups	1. In a mixing bowl, combine 1 1/2 cups of the sugar, tapioca, and spices; mix well.
Quick-cooking tapioca	1 1/8 cups	
Ground cinnamon	2 tablespoons	
Ground cloves	1 1/2 tablespoons	
Ground nutmeg	1 teaspoon	
Milk	3 cups	2. Combine milk with egg yolks; beat well. Pour over sugar mixture; let stand for 10 minutes. Stir in applesauce and lemon juice. Turn mixture into pie shells.
Eggs, separated	12	
Applesauce	4 1/2 quarts	
Lemon juice	3/4 cup	3. Bake in a preheated 375 °F. oven until pie is firm in the center and crust is brown, about 1 hour.
Unbaked pie shells	6	4. Beat egg whites until soft peaks form. Gradually add remaining 1 1/2 cups sugar; beat until stiff but not dry.
		5. Spread meringue over filling, sealing it to edges of pie shells all around.
		6. Increase oven heat to 425 °F. Bake until meringue is browned, about 5 minutes.

Maple Custard Pie

Yield: six 9-inch pies

Featured Seasonings: pure vanilla extract, ground nutmeg, salt, maple syrup, shredded coconut

Ingredients	Quantities	Procedure
Milk, divided	3 3/4 quarts	1. In a large mixing bowl, combine 1 1/2 cups of the milk and cornstarch; blend well. Add eggs; beat well. Stir in vanilla extract, nutmeg, and salt; set aside.
Cornstarch	1/2 cup	
Eggs	24	
Pure vanilla extract	1/4 cup	
Ground nutmeg	4 1/2 teaspoons	
Salt	1 1/2 teaspoons	
Maple syrup	3 cups	2. In a sauce pan, combine syrup with remaining milk. Heat just to the boiling point; gradually stir into the egg mixture; blend well. Pour into pie shells.
Unbaked 9-inch pie shells	6	
Shredded coconut	3 cups	3. Bake in a preheated 450°F. oven for 10 minutes. Reduce heat to 325°F. and bake 30 minutes longer. Sprinkle coconut over custard. Bake 10 minutes longer.
		4. Cool on racks.

Belgian Pears

Yield: 48 portions

Featured Seasonings: coffee, bay leaves, whole cloves, pure vanilla extract, lemon juice

Ingredients	Quantities	Procedure
Large firm pears	48	1. Peel pears, leaving them whole with stems intact.
Water	3 quarts	2. In a large sauce pot, combine water, coffee, sugar, bay leaves, and cloves. Bring to the boiling point. Reduce heat, add pears and poach, covered, until tender, about 30 minutes.
Weak coffee	2 quarts	
Sugar	2 quarts	
Small bay leaves	8	3. Remove pears to a bowl; set aside.
Whole cloves	16	4. Reduce liquid by one half.
Pure vanilla extract	3 tablespoons	5. Stir in vanilla extract and lemon juice. Pour syrup over pears. Chill.
Lemon juice	3 tablespoons	
		6. Serve pears in dessert dishes sauced with syrup.

Sultsinat (Filled Rye Pastries)

Yield: 96 pastries

Featured Seasonings: salt, ground nutmeg, butter, ground cinnamon

Ingredients	Quantities	Procedure
Water	1 1/2 quarts	1. In a bowl combine water, oil, 2 tablespoons of the salt, and 1 teaspoon of the nutmeg. Stir in flours.
Oil	3/4 cup	
Salt, divided	3 tablespoons	2. Turn dough onto a well-floured board; knead until smooth, about 5 minutes.
Ground nutmeg, divided	2 teaspoons	
Rye flour	3 quarts	3. Shape dough into 6 rolls, each 16 inches long. Cut each roll into sixteen 1-inch pieces. On a lightly floured board, roll each piece into a 7-inch circle.
All-purpose flour	7 1/2 cups	
		4. Cook, a few at a time, on an ungreased griddle or large skillet over high heat, about 20 seconds on each side. Stack, keep warm.
Milk, divided	3 3/4 quarts	5. In a sauce pot, combine 3 quarts of the milk with farina, remaining 1 tablespoon salt, and 1 teaspoon nutmeg. Cook and stir for 1 minute.
Quick-cooking farina	3 cups	
Egg yolks	6	6. Combine remaining 3 cups milk with egg yolks. Gradually stir into farina mixture; cook and stir 1 minute longer. Remove from heat; cover and let stand until mixture thickens, about 3 minutes.
Sugar	1 1/2 cups	7. Stir in sugar, butter, and cinnamon.
Butter or margarine	1 1/8 cups	8. Spread 2 to 3 tablespoons farina mixture over each pastry. Roll up.
Ground cinnamon	1/4 cup	
		9. Dust with confectioners sugar and cinnamon, if desired. Serve warm.

Puerto Rican Pudding

Yield: 48 portions

Featured Seasonings: light rum, ground cinnamon, ground nutmeg, ground allspice, ground cloves, salt

Ingredients	Quantities	Procedure
Dark seedless raisins	1 1/2 quarts	1. Soak raisins in the rum for 24 hours or longer.
Light rum	3 cups	
Eggs	18	2. In a mixing bowl, beat eggs until light. Add milk and butter; blend well. Stir in bread crumbs, sugar, spices, and salt. Stir in almonds, the reserved soaked raisins, and any rum remaining in bowl.
Milk	1 1/2 quarts	
Butter or margarine, melted	1 1/2 cups	
Dry bread crumbs	7 1/2 cups	
Sugar	6 cups	3. Turn into six 1 1/2-quart baking pans. Place pans in a large pan with 1 inch hot water.
Ground cinnamon	1/4 cup	
Ground nutmeg	1 tablespoon	4. Bake in a preheated 350°F. oven until pudding is firm, about 1 1/2 hours.
Ground allspice	1 1/2 teaspoons	
Ground cloves	1 1/2 teaspoons	
Salt	1 1/2 teaspoons	
Toasted slivered almonds	1 1/2 quarts	
Spiced Whipped Cream (see following recipe)	3 quarts	5. Serve warm with Spiced Whipped Cream (following recipe).

Spiced Whipped Cream

Yield: 3 quarts

Featured Seasonings: ground cinnamon, grount nutmeg, pure vanilla extract

Ingredients	Quantities	Procedure
Heavy cream	1 1/2 quarts	1. In a mixing bowl, combine 1 1/2 quarts heavy cream, 3/4 cup superfine sugar, 1 1/2 tablespoons ground cinnamon, 1 1/2 teaspoons ground nutmeg, and 2 tablespoons pure vanilla extract.
Sugar, superfine	3/4 cup	
Ground cinnamon	1 1/2 tablespoons	
Ground nutmeg	1 1/2 teaspoons	2. Beat until stiff. Serve with Puerto Rican Pudding.
Pure vanilla extract	2 tablespoons	

Aviz Oranges

Yield: 36 to 48 portions

Featured Seasonings: port wine, ground cinnamon

Ingredients	Quantities	Procedure
Navel oranges	36	1. With vegetable peeler, peel off orange part of skin of 12 of the oranges in long thin strips. Sliver into 1/8-inch wide strips. Place orange slivers in a sauce pan with boiling, salted water to cover; cook until tender; drain and reserve strips.
Water	As directed	
Sugar	1 1/2 quart	2. In the same sauce pan, combine sugar and 3 cups water; bring to the boiling point. Add softened strips; cook until crystallized; reserve for later use.
		3. Peel remaining oranges, removing also white portion of previously peeled oranges. Cut oranges crosswise in 1/4-inch thick slices. Place in glass serving bowls.
Raspberry jelly	3 cups	4. Melt raspberry and guava jellies; stir in port wine and cinnamon. Cool. Pour over oranges and chill.
Guava jelly	3 cups	
Port wine	1 1/2 cups	5. Serve, garnished with crystallized orange peel.
Ground cinnamon	1 tablespoon	

MISCELLANEOUS

Burghul Dolmi
(Persian Minted Cracked Wheat Stuffing)

Yield: 36 cups

Featured Seasonings: butter, celery, onions, mint flakes, salt, ground black pepper, tawny port

Ingredients	Quantities	Procedure
Butter or margarine	1 1/2 cups	1. In a large skillet, melt butter. Add celery and onions; sauté until tender.
Celery, chopped	3 cups	
Onions, chopped	3 cups	
Bulgar (cracked wheat), parboiled	3 quarts	2. Add bulgar; sauté for 5 minutes, stirring constantly.
Apricots, quartered	1 1/8 quarts	3. Stir in apricots, prunes, mint flakes, salt, black pepper, beef broth, port, and water. Simmer, covered, until cracked wheat is tender, 20 to 30 minutes, stirring occasionally.
Prunes, quartered	1 1/8 quarts	
Mint flakes	2 tablespoons	
Salt	4 1/2 teaspoons	
Ground black pepper	1 teaspoon	
Canned condensed beef broth	3 (50 oz.) cans	
Tawny port	1 quart	
Water	3 cups	
Pine nuts, toasted	1 1/2 cups	4. Stir in pine nuts.
		5. Use to stuff poultry or pork chops.

Nimbu Chatni (Indian Date and Lemon Chutney)

Yield: 3 1/2 quarts

Featured Seasonings: salt, ground ginger, ground coriander, ground black pepper, fresh lemon juice, shredded coconut, fennel seeds

Ingredients	Quantities	Procedure
Sugar	1/3 cup	1. In a bowl combine sugar, salt, ginger, coriander, black pepper, and lemon juice. Stir in dates and coconut.
Salt	2 tablespoons	
Ground ginger	4 teaspoons	
Ground coriander	2 teaspoons	
Ground black pepper	1 teaspoon	
Fresh lemon juice	1 cup	
Pitted dates, quartered	4 pounds	
Shredded coconut	1 cup	
Fennel seeds	4 teaspoons	2. Crush fennel seeds; stir into date mixture. Serve at once or cover tightly and refrigerate for 2 to 3 days.
		3. Serve with chicken or fish.

English Potato and Sausage Stuffing

Yield: 12 cups

Featured Seasonings: onion flakes, parsley flakes, sage leaves, salt, ground black pepper

Ingredients	Quantities	Procedure
Onion flakes	1/2 cup	1. Rehydrate onion flakes in water for 10 minutes.
Water	1/3 cup	
Potatoes, peeled and diced	10 cups	2. Cook potatoes in boiling water to cover for 5 minutes. Drain and reserve potatoes, reserving 1/2 cup potato water; set aside.
Pork sausage links, sliced	1 pound	3. In a large skillet, saute sausage, about 5 minutes. Remove and reserve sausage, leaving fat in skillet (about 1/3 cup).
Fresh mushrooms, sliced	1 pound	4. Add rehydrated onion and mushrooms to skillet; saute for 5 minutes.
Butter or margarine	1/4 cup	5. Add butter, seasonings, and reserved potatoes and sausage. Cook and stir for 5 minutes. Turn mixture into a steam table pan.
Parsley flakes	2 tablespoons	
Sage leaves, crumbled	1 teaspoon	
Salt	1 teaspoon	6. Add reserved 1/2 cup potato water to skillet; bring to the boiling point; stir to release particles in bottom of skillet. Pour over stuffing.
Ground black pepper	1 teaspoon	7. Cover and bake in a preheated 325 °F. oven 20 to 30 minutes.

Jalapeno Plunge

Yield: 3 quarts

Featured Seasonings: jalapeno peppers

Ingredients	Quantities	Procedure
Cream cheese, melted	3 pounds	1. In a sauce pan, blend cream cheese with canned tomatoes.
Canned tomatoes, crushed	1 (46 oz.) can	
Jalapeno peppers, finely chopped	To taste	2. Add jalapeno peppers. Heat until hot.
		3. Serve sauce warm with breaded shrimp, breaded scallops, or breaded fish fillets. Garnish with chopped parsley, if desired.

Chick Pea Spread

Yield: 4 1/2 cups

Featured Seasonings: lemon juice, onion powder, garlic powder, paprika, salt, ground black pepper

Ingredients	Quantities	Procedure
Canned chick peas	2 (20 oz.) cans	1. Mash chick peas.
Olive or salad oil	1 1/3 cups	2. Stir in oil, lemon juice, onion powder, garlic powder, paprika, salt, and black pepper. Cover and refrigerate.
Lemon juice	1/4 cup	
Onion powder	1 tablespoon	3. Use as a spread on bread or crackers, if desired.
Garlic powder	1 1/2 teaspoons	
Paprika	1 1/2 teaspoons	
Salt	1 1/2 teaspoons	
Ground black pepper	1/2 teaspoon	

Anchovy Butter

Yield: 1 3/4 quart

Featured Seasonings: butter, lemon juice, chopped parsley, anchovy paste, salt, ground black pepper

Ingredients	Quantities	Procedure
Butter	1 pound	1. In a heavy pot, melt butter. Stir in flour; cook and stir over low heat 2 to 3 minutes.
Flour	1/4 cup	
Beef stock or water	1 quart	2. Stir in remaining ingredients. Bring to a boil; reduce heat and simmer for 5 minutes, stirring frequently.
Lemon juice	1/2 cup	
Parsley, chopped	1/2 cup	3. Serve over fish or vegetables.
Anchovy paste	1/3 cup	
Salt	1 tablespoon	
Ground black pepper	1 teaspoon	

Plum Sauce

Yield:	4 1/2 quarts
Featured Seasoning:	chutney

Ingredients	Quantities	Procedure
Plum preserves	1 (No. 10) can	1. Combine plum preserves and chutney; add sugar to taste. Heat until hot.
Chutney	6 cups	
Sugar	To taste	2. Serve warm with breaded fish, scallops, shrimp, etc.

Creamy Horseradish Sauce

Yield: 2 quarts

Featured Seasonings: horseradish, sour cream, dill

Ingredients	Quantities	Procedure
Bottled horseradish, drained	1 quart	1. Blend horseradish with sour cream; cover and chill.
Dairy sour cream	1 quart	
Fresh dill, finely chopped	As desired	2. Serve sauce cold, topped with fresh dill with fried shrimp, breaded scallops, fish fillets, etc.

Peanut Buttery Vegetable Sauce

Yield: 2 1/2 quarts

Featured Seasonings: butter, salt, ground black pepper

Ingredients	Quantities	Procedure
Butter or margarine	1/2 cup	1. In a sauce pan melt butter; blend in peanut butter. Add flour and seasonings; stir until smooth. Slowly stir in milk.
Peanut butter	2 cups	
Flour	1/3 cup	2. Cook over low heat, stirring constantly, until thickened.
Salt	4 teaspoons	3. Serve over cooked vegetables like broiled tomatoes, Brussels sprouts, cauliflower buds, carrot slices, peas on toast points.
Ground black pepper	1 teaspoon	
Milk	2 quarts	

Sauce a la Russe

Yield: 48 portions

Featured Seasonings: butter, parsley flakes, chervil leaves, tarragon leaves, powdered mustard, ground white pepper, lemon juice

Ingredients	Quantities	Procedure
Butter or margarine	1 cup	1. In a small sauce pan, melt butter. Stir in flour; cook and stir for 2 minutes. Stir in chicken broth. Cook and stir until mixture boils and thickens.
Flour	1 cup	
Canned condensed chicken broth	2 (50 oz.) cans	
Parsley flakes	3 tablespoons	2. Stir in parsley, chervil, tarragon, mustard, white pepper, and lemon juice. Heat until hot.
Chervil leaves, crumbled	3 tablespoons	
Tarragon leaves, crumbled	4 teaspoons	3. Serve over beef or poultry.
Powdered mustard	2 teaspoons	
Ground white pepper	1 teaspoon	
Lemon juice	3 tablespoons	

Virgin Island Curry Sauce

Featured Seasonings: onions, celery, butter, curry powder, ground ginger, bay leaves, salt, ground black pepper, coconut milk, lime juice

Ingredients	Quantities	Procedure
Butter or margarine	1/2 cup	1. In a medium sauce pan, melt butter. Add onions and celery; sauté for 3 minutes.
Onions, minced	1 cup	
Celery, chopped	1 cup	
Curry powder	1/2 cup	2. Stir in curry powder and ginger. Cook and stir for 1 minute. Add flour; cook and stir 1 minute longer.
Ground ginger	2 teaspoons	
Flour	1/4 cup	
Canned condensed beef broth	1 (50 oz.) can	3. Stir in beef broth, bay leaves, salt, and black pepper. Bring to the boiling point. Reduce heat and simmer, uncovered, for 1 minute.
Bay leaves	4	
Salt	2 teaspoons	
Ground black pepper	1/2 teaspoon	
Coconut milk or light cream	1 quart	4. Stir in coconut milk and lime juice. Heat until hot. Remove bay leaves.
Lime juice	1 tablespoon	
		5. Serve over chicken.

Italian White Clam Sauce

Yield: 3 quarts

Featured Seasonings: olive oil, butter, onions, garlic, parsley flakes, basil leaves, salt, ground black pepper

Ingredients	Quantities	Procedure
Olive oil	1 1/2 cups	1. In a sauce pot, heat oil and butter. Add onions and garlic; sauté for 5 minutes.
Butter or margarine	1 1/2 cups	
Onions, minced	1 1/2 cups	
Garlic, minced	1/4 cup	
Canned minced clams	6 (10 1/2 oz.) cans	2. Drain clams, reserving liquid; set clams aside.
Bottled clam juice	6 (8 oz.) bottles	3. To sautéed onions and garlic, add clam liquid and juice, parsley, basil, salt, and black pepper. Simmer, uncovered, for 5 minutes.
Parsley flakes	3/4 cup	
Basil leaves, crushed	1/4 cup	
Salt	1 1/2 teaspoons	4. Stir in reserved clams. Heat until hot. Pour over hot cooked spaghetti.
Ground black pepper	3/4 teaspoon	

Swedish Mustard Sauce

Yield: 5 cups

Featured Seasonings: white vinegar, powdered mustard, salt, ground white pepper, ground cardamom seeds

Ingredients	Quantities	Procedure
Oil	3 cups	1. In a medium bowl, combine all ingredients. Beat with a wire whip until thickened, about 1 minute.
White vinegar	3/4 cup	2. Serve with ham or fish.
Sugar	1 1/3 cups	
Powdered mustard	1/3 cup	
Salt	5 teaspoons	**Note:** This sauce remains thick and emulsified without further stirring.
Ground white pepper	1 teaspoon	
Ground cardamom seeds	1 teaspoon	

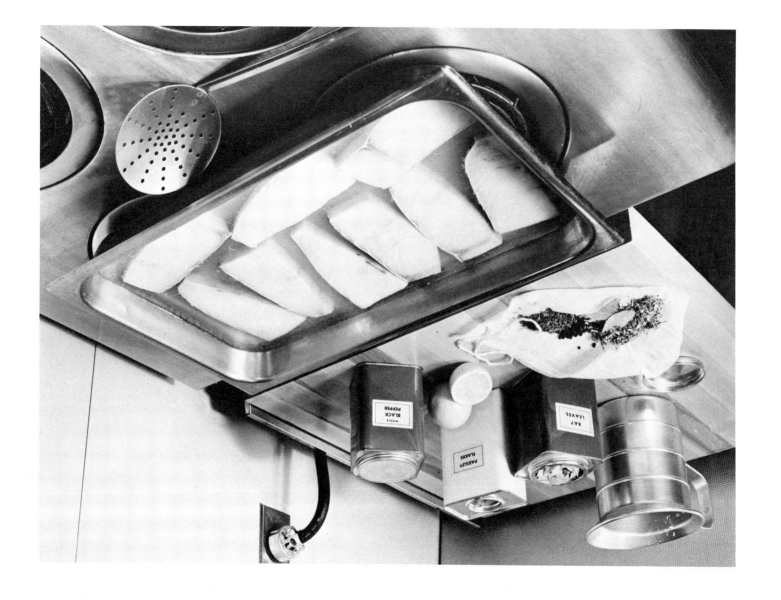

Court Bouillon for Fish and Shellfish

Yield: 1 gallon

Featured Seasonings: onion flakes, celery flakes, parsley flakes, bay leaves, whole black pepper, thyme leaves, white or cider vinegar, lemon, salt

Ingredients	Quantities	Procedure
Onion flakes	3/4 cup	1. Tie onion, celery, and parsley flakes, bay leaves, black pepper, and thyme in a cheesecloth bag.
Celery flakes	1/4 cup	
Parsley flakes	1/4 cup	
Bay leaves	4	
Whole black pepper	2 tablespoons	
Thyme leaves	2 teaspoons	
Water	1 gallon	2. In a large pot combine water, vinegar, lemon, and salt; bring to the boiling point. Add spice bag. Simmer, covered, for 20 minutes. Remove spice bag and lemon slices.
White or cider vinegar	1 cup	
Lemon, thinly sliced	1	
Salt	3 tablespoons	3. Use court bouillon as needed for poaching fish and shellfish and for flavoring soups and sauces.

Rouille Sauce

Yield: 4 cups

Featured Seasonings: green peppers, garlic, crushed red pepper, whole pimientos

Ingredients	Quantities	Procedure
Green peppers, chopped	2 cups	1. In a small sauce pan, combine green peppers, garlic, red pepper, and water; bring to the boiling point. Reduce heat and simmer, uncovered, for 3 minutes. Strain through a fine sieve.
Garlic, minced	2 tablespoons	
Crushed red pepper	1 teaspoon	
Water	1 quart	
Oil	2 cups	2. Place in the jar of an electric blender with oil and pimientoes. Blend until smooth, about 1 minute.
Whole pimientoes	4	
Fine dry bread crumbs	1/4 cup	3. Stir in bread crumbs until combined.
		4. Serve with fish steaks, if desired.

Additional Reading on Seasonings

The Art of Cooking with Herbs & Spices. Milo Miloradovich. Doubleday & Co., Inc., Garden City, N.Y., 1950.

The Book of Herbs. Lady Rosalind Northcote. (Originally published in 1903). Reprint. Dover Publications, New York, 1971.

The Book of Spices. Frederic Rosengarten, Jr. Livingston Press, Philadelphia, 1969.

The Clove Tree. G. E. Tidbury. Crosby Lockwood & Son, Ltd., London, 1949.

Colloquies of the Simples and Drugs of India. Garcia da Orta. Henry Sotheran & Co., London, 1913. (Modern translation).

Culpeper's Complete Herbal. Nicholas Culpeper. (Originally published in 1652). Reprint. W. Foulsham & Co., Ltd., London, n. d.

Das Buch des Gewurze. Roland Goock. Mosaik Verlag, Hamburg, Germany, 1965. (Only available in German).

Dictionary of the Economic Products of the Malay Peninsula. I. H. Burkill. Crown Agents for the Colonies, London, 1935.

The Dispensatory of the United States of America. Arthur Osol and H. C. Wood. J. B. Lippincott Co., Philadelphia, 1943.

Garden Spice & Wild Pot Herbs. W. C. Muenscher and M. A. Rice. Cornell University Press, Ithaca, N.Y., 1955.

Greek Herbal of Dioscorides. Edited by Robert T. Gunther. Oxford University Press, Oxford, 1934.

Herbal. John Gerarde. (Originally published in 1636). Reprint. Spring Books, London, 1964.

Herbal Delights. Mrs. C. F. Leyel. Houghton Mifflin Co., Boston, 1938.

Herbs, Health, & Cookery. Phillippa Back and Claire Loewenfeld. Hawthorn Books, New York, 1967.

Herbs, Spices and Flavorings. Tom Stobart. McGraw-Hill Book Company, New York, 1970.

Herbs, Their Culture and Uses. Rosetta Clarkson. The MacMillan Co., New York, 1942.

In Quest of Spices. Sonia E. Howe. Herbert Jenkins, Ltd., London, 1946.

Modern Herbal. Mrs. M. Grieve. 2 vols. Reprint. Dover Publications, New York, 1971. Paperback.

Of Spices and Herbs. Colin Clair. Abelard Schuman, London, 1961.

Pepper and Pirates. James Duncan Phillips. The Riverside Press, Cambridge, Mass., 1949.

Perfumes & Spices. A. Hyatt Verrill. L. C. Page & Co., Boston, 1940.

Plant Lore, Legends and Lyrics. Richard Folkhard, Jr. Sampson Low, London, 1892.

The Spice Cookbook. Avanelle Day and Lillie Stuckey. David White Co., New York, 1964.

Spices. Henry N. Ridley. The MacMillan Co., New York, 1912.

Spices, Vol. 1. The Story of Spices. J. W. Parry. Chemical Publishing Co., New York, 1969.

Spices, Vol. 2. Morphology, Histology & Chemistry. J. W. Parry. Chemical Publishing Co., New York, 1969.

Spices and Condiments. Stanley Redgrove. Isaac Pitman Co., London, 1933.

Spices and Herbs Around the World. Elizabeth S. Hayes. Doubleday & Co., Garden City, N.Y., 1961.

Spices, Salt and Aromatics in the English Kitchen. Elizabeth David. Penguin Books, Middlesex, England, 1970.

Sturtevant's Notes on Edible Plants. Edited by U. P. Hedrick. J. B. Lyons Co., State Printers, Albany, N.Y., 1919.

Sumatra—America's Pepperpot. James W. Gould. Essex Institute Historical Collections, Salem, Mass., April, July, October, 1956.

Index

273